A TENBY LIFEBOAT FAMILY

Contents

SACRED GROUND	7
LIFE IN LONDON	8
ARRIVAL IN TENBY	14
FERMANAGH RESCUE	21
LIFEBOATMAN POEM	31
TENBY LIFEBOAT HEROES	32
TENBY LIFEBOAT ROLL OF HONOUR	57
ONE OF THE MOST BEAUTIFUL	58
HE CALLED ME HIS MONA LISA	62
THE WAR	72
TENBY ROLL OF HONOUR	87
PEMBROKE DOCK IN THE BLITZ	96
PEMBROKE DOCK ROLL OF HONOUR	102
TENBY WOMEN AT WAR	106
VE DAY IN TENBY	125
THEN FISH AND CHIPS AT FECCI'S	126
SCOTSBOROUGH HOUSE	128
MY BEST FRIEND WAS WENDY	130
SHANLY'S SOUTH BEACH PAVILION	138
SAINT MARGARET'S FAIR	147
THE CIRCUS COMES TO TOWN	149
GYPSIES OF KILGETTY COMMON	155
ROYAL INFLUENCES	165
SAD FAREWELL TO TENBY	171
BUILDING ON SHIFTING SANDS	181
HAPPY REUNIONS	191
EPILOGUE	199

*(**Publisher's note:** It is the long-term intention of the author to attempt to publish an expanded version of this book in an illustrated hardback edition. Displays of **Tenby Lifeboat** memorabilia can be viewed at **Tenby Lifeboat Station** and at **Tenby Museum**.)*

Also available as
Star of Pembrokeshire
series paperbacks ...

PRESELI BLUESTONES
BY
SION PYSGOD

ISBN 0-9533512-0-3

WESTERN TELEGRAPH: *"Tenby-born author turns redundancy into publishing venture ... the philosophy of the company is the publication of modern Welsh literature with a Pembrokeshire theme written by local authors"*

TENBY OBSERVER: *"In what is believed to be a World First for Wales, the novel Preseli Bluestones has been simultaneously published in paperback and on the Internet via the publisher's Preseli Bluestones Internet Subscription Channel"*

ATLAS-LINKS NEWS: *"Preseli Bluestones is a science fiction novel featuring aspects of Pembrokeshire's history and folklore, so exploring Pembrokeshire's relationship with Stonehenge via the Bluestones of the Preseli Mountains"*

Signed First Edition
June 2000

STAR OF PEMBROKESHIRE SERIES

Best Wishes

A TENBY LIFEBOAT FAMILY

the memoirs in her own words of Tenby Lifeboatman's daughter

AVIS NIXON
(née COTTAM)

Avis Nixon (née Cottam)

Includes the author's poem
The Lifeboatman
A tribute to the Tenby Lifeboat

PUBLISHED IN THE PEMBROKESHIRE COASTAL NATIONAL PARK

2 A TENBY LIFEBOAT FAMILY

First published 2000 by
John Fish B.Sc. Publishers of Tenby in Wales
simultaneously in a Star of Pembrokeshire series paperback edition
and in an online edition on the publisher's
Preseli Bluestones Internet Subscription Channel
that can be accessed from the publisher's homepage:

http://homepages.which.net/~j.fish/
e-mail: j.fish@which.net

ISBN 0-9533512-2-X

Copyright © 2000 Avis Nixon
Dedicated to my late father Tenby Lifeboatman Alfred Cottam and to all Tenby Lifeboatmen past, present and future.

Acknowledgement: the author would like to acknowledge the permission of **Jeff Morris** (Honorary Archivist of the RNLI) for allowing her to use his illustrated book **Tenby Lifeboats** as the foundation of the chapter entitled **Tenby Lifeboat Heroes**. (Refer to page 32 for details of how to obtain this book.)

Cover design (including Star of Pembrokeshire logo) typesetting, pagination, proof-reading and copy-editing by John Fish B.Sc. State of the art desktop publishing utilising Microsoft Word 97.

Printed in Pembrokeshire by
CIT Printing Services of Haverfordwest

All rights reserved. No part of this book may be reproduced by any photographic, mechanical or electronic process, or as an audio recording, nor stored in any type of memory system, transmitted or copied for private or public use without the written permission of the publishers. This book being sold on condition that it shall not be repackaged by the purchaser, in any form whatsoever, with any subsequent purchaser similarly conditioned, without the written permission of the publishers.

The publishers are members of Pembrokeshire County Council's Pembrokeshire Produce Mark scheme
www.pembrokeshire.gov.uk

A TENBY LIFEBOAT FAMILY 5

SILLY MID OFF
BY
DAVE AINSWORTH

ISBN 0-9533512-1-1

TENBY OBSERVER: *"Silly Mid Off is a comedy novel firmly rooted in modern Pembrokeshire ... funny, well crafted and keeps you hooked right to the very end ... some truly laugh-out-loud moments, but also pathos and poignancy ... Silly Mid Off will bowl you over!"*

WESTERN TELEGRAPH: *"Comedian turned teacher scores with cricket novel ... legendary Landsker Cup ... packed with humour ... with a racy style ... a sub-plot concentrates on an amateur dramatics performance of Shakespeare's 'A Midsummer's Night Dream' at Carew Castle."*

WESTERN MAIL: *"A gentle racy romp in the Tom Sharpe mould ... clever set pieces ... bowls along at an enjoyable lick ... Ainsworth has a good eye for character ... take great delight in spotting all the Pembrokeshire landmarks that crop up ... background as a stand-up comedian shines through in his shrewd observations on human deviousness."*

*(**Publisher's note**: Star of Pembrokeshire series paperbacks can be ordered from any UK bookshop via the Welsh Books Council and worldwide through the Internet at www.amazon.co.uk)*

AUTHORS ACKNOWLEDGEMENTS

My heartfelt thanks to the Tenby Branch of the Royal National Lifeboat Institution: Coxswain Alan Thomas, Wyn Griffiths and crew of the Tenby Lifeboat for their interest and warm welcome: Honorary President Eric Bancroft whose very generous help and encouragement made this book possible: Honorary Secretary Arthur Squibbs for his humour and friendly letters full of news and help with my researches: Jeff Morris' detailed record entitled Tenby Lifeboats proved an invaluable reference, his work is available through Tenby Lifeboat outlets and Tenby bookshops: RNLI headquarters in Poole and Tenby RNLI for their approval of this project.

Tenby Museum and Art Gallery: Curator John Beynon, Assistant Curator Deborah Wildgust and Museum Officer Mark Lewis for all their hard work on my behalf; given in an interested, friendly and generous way over a period of years.

Paterchurch Publications, Pembroke Dock (aviation and maritime specialist publishers): John and Christine Evans for their help and friendship.

Tenby's www.atlas-links.com Internet Community: Alan Brindley, Harry Smith, Martin Lees-Griffths and Fred Wildgust for helping to make a dream come true.

Pembrokeshire County Council: Cultural Services' Officer Mrs Mary John for reviewing my work and recommending it as suitable for student research.

Alastair Macarthur of Stone, Staffordshire: the son of John Macarthur who was rescued by the Tenby Lifeboat whilst a crewman of the SS Fermanagh in 1938: thank you Alastair for all your help and correspondence over the years, our parents' lives were entwined by fate.

The Rector of Tenby Canon David Jenkins for permission to publish the Tenby Roll of Honour with assistance from Wilf Hardy, President of Tenby Royal British Legion.

Pembroke Dock Town Council: Town Clerk Mrs W A Vincent for her help in my research and permission to publish the Pembroke Dock Roll of Honour.

To all my family and friends who have read and reviewed my manuscript; to Stanley Speight, Chairperson of Tenby Local History Society, and Mrs Nesta Fish for 'local knowledge.'

A TENBY LIFEBOAT FAMILY

the memoirs in her own words of Tenby Lifeboatman's daughter

AVIS NIXON
(née Cottam)

SACRED GROUND

My letter to the Tenby Observer of 30th October 1998:

Dear Sir,
 With regard to plans for a new Tenby Lifeboat House and Slip as reported in the Tenby Observer.

My father, Alfred Cottam, was the Mechanic of the Tenby Lifeboat from 1933 to 1948.

Behind each brave and dedicated Lifeboatman there is a family. In our case seven children.

The small income he received kept us on the poverty line, shoes with holes, no socks in winter, no gloves, no rainwear, one small fire to warm the house. We huddled three to a bed to keep warm.

Blessed with our beautiful surroundings, kind neighbours and many friends, we were happy and proud of our father.

After many years of coping with the hardship, our pretty mother gave up and left us. After 1948 we never saw our father again.

We do not know where he died or was buried.

Exiles now scattered across the world we return like pilgrims to the Tenby Lifeboat House to honour our father and ease our loss.

We are just one Tenby Lifeboat family of that time. There were John Williams, George Hooper, Benjamin Richards, William Thomas, Ivor Crockford, John Rees, Frank Hooper, Bertie Lewis, Fred Harries, Alexander Harries, Thomas E Lewis, their families, and many more before and since.

Can you imagine what it means to them personally? It is on par with destroying the War Memorial which stands to remind us of our other brave townsmen.

Have your new Lifeboat House and Slip – too good a chance to miss - but please try to keep the old one, even if part of the Slip has to go.

Without our roots none of us has any future or sense of belonging.

In today's society where money is the main God, treasure the high principles of your good townsmen, Lifeboatmen, one generation after another of the same families who give the ultimate a man can give, the risk of their lives to save others.

>Yours Sincerely,
>Avis Nixon (née Cottam)
>Tenby Lifeboatman's daughter.

LIFE IN LONDON

My father Alfred Cottam, only child of a mother who we never met, and a father never spoken of, was born in 1895 in Middlesborough.

His mother, who was devoted to him, put her handsome and intelligent son to a naval career. He became a communications' officer and served in submarines in their early days. On one fateful dive, the submarine burst its sides. They managed to surface and were eventually rescued by the Lifeboat. My father vowed then that in return for his life he would devote his working life at sea to saving others.

He had navigation qualifications and was also a marine engineer and radio operator. He had met my mother when on leave in London. She lived in Millwall, one of sixteen children. He had taken lodgings in the house next door. My mother Annie Ethel Webb was very pretty, she had auburn curly hair, blue eyes, slim build with beautiful skin. My father was tall, dark and handsome and they fell passionately in love. So much so that they had made love before he went back to sea, and on his next leave they married as my mother had fallen for a baby.

When you write of things that happened sixty odd years ago you realise how things have changed in our society. In this family story we have to remember that our parents were descended from the Victorian era and had all those inhibitions instilled in them. What a great part this plays in their lives. It was therefore unusual that my mother when talking to her daughters told us quite openly that she was pregnant when she married and wore a pretty pleated cape to conceal it. We just accepted it without question.

My eldest sister Dora Elaine was born in 1922. A very pretty baby, a replica of my mother except that she would grow much taller.

In 1925 my mother gave birth to her second daughter Joyce Adelaide, nearly eleven pounds in weight, full set of teeth and thick black curls - quite a baby. Despite the birth pains my mother must have endured she named her Joy, and what joy she has brought to those who have known her great love and loyalty.

Another two years hence mother had her third daughter Margaret Rose called Peggy. Fair, slight and ethereal with the sweetest of natures but with an inner strength none attributed to her until her adversities in later life.

My sister Barbara Jacqueline came along as a matter of course two years later. Another big baby with dark curls and a happy loving nature, bit of a tomboy but very maternal.

Keeping to her fertile pattern mother's fifth daughter was Beryl Gwendoline Mary, nine and a half pounds in weight and a mass of fair curls. Another tomboy with a strong maternal instinct. This was a difficult time for mother as her health failed her. She had pleurisy and phlebitis as well as the birth to contend with along with five children in a London flat. My father was at sea most of the time and his money did not always come through. Mother got involved with a money-lender in order to feed the family.

The elder girls had to answer the door to callers and take bedding and clothing to the pawnshop regularly. They then had only coats on their beds to keep them warm and more often than not not enough food to eat. The flat they lived in looked over the East India Docks. Only the living room floor boasted lino floor covering, the other rooms were bare boards. Times were hard, they like many others were caught in the poverty trap.

Dora was like a little mother to the younger ones, as was expected of her. One day she had been sent on an errand (dad had been doing some work in the hall standing on a chair) and she fell, and banged her knee very badly but had to limp away on her errand. In our home children did as they were told regardless. After a few weeks her knee was still very swollen and stiff. It was discovered that she had an inner abscess and had to go to Great Ormond Street Children's Hospital and have the leg operated on. This left her with a long scar on her inner leg.

On a happier note for the children, there was a park opposite the flat that they could play in. The park attendant was a friendly man, when they sat on the big long swing together he sang the old Cockney song to them: "Ain't it grand to be blooming well dead." Just the thing for little children, but they loved it and him.

Joyce longed for a doll's pram. The park attendant said he'd buy her a doll and a pram one day. Working class people were so poor, a roof over their heads and food in their bellies was the most they could hope for and afford. Clothes were well worn, only replaced when in pieces and then by second-hand garments.

Trouble with a woman money-lender occurred one memorable day. She called at the flat for her money payment which mother didn't have. Afraid after repeated loud knocks mother told the children to hide under the table. The woman started shouting through the letterbox: "I know you're in there." Thinking of the neighbours, mother took courage and opened the door, quick as a flash the woman struck out like a man and punched her in the face. She had gold sovereign rings on her fingers, which made the blood pour down mother's face. The children were crying and so afraid. The woman took mother by the hair and dragged her into the street, where she left her, jumped on her cart, whipped the horse and off she went. The children had to help mother in and bathe her face. At a later date mother took the woman to Court for assault, but being so poor they were so vulnerable.

When you don't have very much, your health is your greatest asset. Their hardiness taken for granted by most. When Beryl was born and mother had pleurisy and phlebitis, father had an accident on one of the ships and broke his ankle. He was hopping about the flat; mother was in bed ill, forbidden to move a finger in case of blood clots. The midwife attending to the baby had not tested the bath water and put Beryl into a very hot bath, blistering her bottom. Dora the eldest was to stay and look after the three invalids, and Joyce, Peggy and Barbara were sent to Grandma Webb's house to ease the domestic situation. She did not really want them, and Joyce became upset, it was her first time away from home, and nerves took over, to the extent that she stated that she couldn't walk. No matter how they enticed her, she couldn't walk. Mum's sister Olive carried her to the shop and bought her some sweets, a rare treat. Still she couldn't walk. Grandma Webb was obviously worried, as she had Joyce in her bed that night. One of Joyce's problems was a weak bladder, she wanted to go to the toilet in the night. The toilet was at the bottom of the garden. Joyce just got out of the bed and went. Grandma Webb was not amused. The next morning they were all packed off back home. Joyce didn't know if it was fright or insecurity or what it was, but it was not a childish trick, they were too strictly brought up for that. She just could not walk.

During this time in London Joyce doesn't remember any unkindness or beatings, they were to come later.

Father had joined the Royal National Lifeboat Institution (RNLI) as a Marine Engineer. He was sent to work short-term in Aldeburgh, Suffolk. The family were to go with him for their first seaside holiday.

They made the journey with dad by sea. On a big boat this was quite a long journey, down the Thames along the Kent and Essex coasts into the North Sea, to Suffolk. It must have been quite rough as they were all seasick. Ill luck did seem to dog them.

They stayed in a boarding house on the sea front but as the children developed whooping cough, which was highly infectious, they were asked to leave to protect the other guests. They spent the rest of the holiday in the sail-loft of a boathouse on the beach. Sleeping on ropes with old canvas sails covering them, coughing their hearts out, they were glad when it was time to go home. Only then they were all sick again.

They must have been brave as they did have a second holiday during their time in London. This time the destination was Margate, also because of the Lifeboat. It was nice and sunny weather and they spent their days on the beach. Joyce found a silver sixpence in the sand, quite a lot of money in those days. Mother asked her to give it to her to buy food for them but Joyce wanted to buy mother a gift, which she did, just some silly trifle.

They once had an unexpected treat when at Christmas they went to the cinema and whilst queuing to get in, a charitable person gave each child a big Jaffa orange and a marzipan fish. They thought this wonderful.

Joyce had made friends with some Jewish children at school and was invited into their home to play. One day she was frightened as their father came home and chased the mother around the table with a carving knife. For what reason as a child she did not know, but mother did not allow her to go there again.

Father had received a posting through the RNLI to go to the Tenby Lifeboat Station (in Pembrokeshire, South-West Wales) as a mechanic. The position also entailed maintaining the Lifeboat and Boathouse full-time. It is the only paid position, as the rest of the crew are volunteers.

He was to find a suitable house in the town for his family, the rent for which would be paid by the RNLI and then deducted from his wages.

Laston House in Castle Square, overlooking Carmarthen Bay and next to the Lifeboat Station along the Castle Hill's cliff top pathway, was available and though well positioned for him he did not think it suitable for the children; he could see them falling over the courtyard wall into the sea. Four new houses had just been built in Broadwell Hayes so he chose one of those. Maudlin Villa was a semi-detached property with a drive at the side, a long garden for the children to play in and to grow vegetables and fruit to help feed them.

Suddenly the children found they were moving, from the only home they had known, they were to go on a long train journey - their first ever - to live in a new place.

On the morning of the departure, Joyce went over to the park to tell her friend the park attendant that she would have to have her doll and pram now as she was leaving. She was looking for him when Peggy called her and said, "You have to come home now Joyce we are leaving." Joyce thought that she would never get her doll and pram now and sad to say she never did get a doll's pram, none of us did. The most we aspired to was the rusty old frame of a pushchair, the wheels of which had been taken off to make a go-cart for our yet to be born brother Alan.

ARRIVAL IN TENBY

But life held more wonders in store for these children. Toys are only objects. Joyce doesn't remember much about the beginning of the journey on the train except that she seemed to fall about a lot with the movement, much to mother's amusement, she could giggle like a young girl at times which endeared her to us. However, after travelling all day they neared Tenby, and it was springtime and all the primroses were out on the railway embankment, she thought how wonderful it was to see all the green fields and trees.

They didn't know then that the garden of their new house went right down to the railway embankment, and in the future years their little feet trod a steep path down to it. They spent many happy hours at the fence watching the trains go by - and they were quite few and far between in those days. They would wave to the engine driver and guard, and excitedly shouting pretend that it was a ghost train. In naïveté they imagined that the smoke from the funnel rose up to form the clouds in the sky. All is imagination at that age of innocence, and what a blessing it is that we experience it.

In future childhood years they enjoyed the railway embankment to the full. Walking along it to the Folly Woods and fields where they could pick fresh mushrooms for mum. Tiny wild strawberries grew in the gullies. Lush blackberries on the brambles, they picked them by the basketful. Mother made jam and wine for Christmas. The wine was made in a large earthenware crock with toasted bread covered with yeast on top to ferment it.

They thought their new house and garden so exciting and spacious. The furniture van had not arrived so they had to sleep on bare floorboards the first night. But they were happy: the future showed promise, lots of exciting things to do. Pickfords delivered the furniture the next day. All long distance drivers in those days only drove so far, stopped overnight somewhere and continued the next day.

The house had three bedrooms and a bathroom upstairs. The landing and stairs were enhanced with a mahogany banister rail, and two side windows on the staircase made it nice and light. In the hallway the front door and side panels were inset with coloured glass, the sunlight sent such pretty patterns through them. The front sitting room had a bay window and window seat, and an oak surround fireplace with nice tiles. The rear living room had a Chatenette grate in the hearth with an oven, hotplate and backboiler. It was a lifeline on many occasions. The kitchen at the end of the hall had a red tiled floor, the sink was below the window, a large gas cooker and a pantry which ran back under the stairs. Outside, two side doors revealed a coal shed and outside toilet. Two toilets for this impoverished family was unbelievable luxury.

The garden was on a raised level from the house. It ran a long way back and had trees within the area, uncultivated as yet as the house had been built in a field.

How our parents came by their furniture, as they were so poor, I do not know (I was yet to be born) but it all came from London. It was all good quality and the only furniture we ever had. I feel it must have been bought with this house in mind. Perhaps dad had an allowance for this or they bought it on weekly payments, I don't know. There were two dining-room suites, two three-piece suites, two double bedroom suites and one single bed. Additionally two chiming clocks, some pictures and mirrors along with two square carpets, lino and stair carpet in a Turkish pattern of red and blue. The makings were there for a happy restart to life, a comfortable home in beautiful surroundings.

Somehow mother seemed out of her depth. They could never get her to come to the beach or the woods with them. She liked the garden, grew crops and talked to the neighbours. Tenby held out her welcoming arms to this well-mannered family, and the love that it instilled has lasted in our hearts all of our lives, and been consolation through our many hardships. Do beautiful places make beautiful people? I'm sure that they do.

The children of school age, Dora, Joyce and Peggy went to Tenby Council School in Greenhill Road [which in 1961 became Tenby County Primary School then in 1979 Saint Teilo Catholic Primary School; a new State School, Tenby County Junior School, having been built in 1977 on the outskirts of the town in Heywood Lane]. It was just a short walk from home down the Maudlins, across the Green and up Greenhill Road to the school. They liked the school. The classroom walls on the playground side, were partitions of wood and glass which were folded back in summer to let the sunshine in - what an innovation in those days.

The headmaster Ossie Morgan, was a strict man, and all in school were in awe of him. Discipline was tight and any break from it meant the cane, which he alone administered. Any child stepping out of line was sent to stand outside his room. Until dealt with ... this alone was a punishment. In retrospect I feel it was the best upbringing a child could have. Underneath we knew him to be a fair and kindly man who had a love of little children. During the War he had evacuees living in his own home. His example was reflected in his staff and children.

We did have one bully teacher, who shall be nameless. It caused amusement on one occasion when walking home for

ARRIVAL IN TENBY 17

lunch. This same teacher was walking in front of us so we were aware of our behaviour, as most teachers appeared to have eyes in the back of their heads. Suddenly one pupil's mother, a large dark-haired lady whose son he had mistreated came down her path. She caught hold of him by the scruff of the neck and punched him in the face. We all ran and hid behind a wall, stuffing our cardigans in our mouths to stop the giggles. It nearly ended in a smack for us as we were late home for lunch, and it was 'bones' as we called it, neck of lamb stew.

In our cutlery drawer there was a teaspoon with a crest on it of the King's head. This was highly sought after by us children. On one lunch-time coming home, Beryl was very piously knelt in Prayer in the porch, "Please God let me have the spoon with the King's head." Barbara stepped over her and got it, such is life!

Our neighbours were so kind, and ranged across the social scale, from the so-called slums of San Domingo [now, with the old National School, the site of the multi-storey car-park] to the proprietors of Tenby's T P Hughes' department store, then Mayor and Mayoress, and Mrs Gibbons of Heywood Lane, and the Simons who had us into their lovely home to play with John who was to die so tragically in a plane accident. Mr Billings who had a picture framing shop in town, become to us a personal Father Christmas, as each year we found a sack on the doorstep with an orange, apple and new penny for each child; associated with the Lifeboat he had made friends with dad.

Dad was very clever with radios and could build one from scratch with his collection of spare parts. So he used to repair Mr Billing's and other townspeople's radios. In those days the case of a radio was made of highly polished wood and as dad's only transport was a bicycle with a little metal carrier over the back wheel, he had to take great care of them. Each radio was stitched into a sacking cover and strapped onto the carrier. Brought home to be repaired on the living room table, much to mother's aggravation as all evening she had to listen to 'whines and twiddles' or the smell of solder, the soldering iron was heated in the fire. As the table boasted a red plush cloth with tassels, we children often crept under it, and imagined we were in a strange craft, with all the noises above our heads. Dad was a creative man, well educated, and earned a few shillings with this hobby, but any poor person who said they couldn't pay him were just told to forget it.

Like everyone our father had many facets to his nature. He expected us children to be obedient, well-mannered, well-spoken, kind to each other and caring. Our table manners were second to none, and we have all grown up to be grateful for this, as we were readily accepted anywhere to set an example to the other children. Regardless of our scruffy clothing and I'm sure not clean limbs at times.

My sister Joyce encountered cruelty from father on some occasions. As she would be beaten by him with his leather belt. Once so hard that she bled. He must have realised that he had exceeded himself as she was bandaged and kept in bed for a week. Dad had been a ship's doctor at some stage of his career, and all our ills were treated by him. The only person to have a doctor who had to be paid for was mother - plus of course the midwife had to be paid for in those pre-NHS days. Obviously distressed at the time Joyce can't make sense of this behaviour, as her wrong doings were minor - coming home late from school. She feels mother was the instigator. When late home she would say, "Wait till your father comes home." Send her to undress until she was naked, and wait for her punishment, which was sometimes a long time as in summer dad would be showing visitors around the Lifeboat Station until nine o'clock.

She [Joyce] feels that this was some twist in mother's genes. In those days the father always metered out the punishment, the stick or the belt was not uncommon, but this was bordering on abuse and should never have happened in a well-balanced household. It hurts me to relate it as I have no wish to think ill of my father, who was my hero and has remained so, but this is a factual family story and it has to be told. It left an emotional scar on a dear sister, if not a bodily one.

By now it is 1935 and I the sixth girl was born on 2nd October. With this event, as with all I have previously written, I only know details from what the elder girls can remember. After all the daughters it seems my mother would have preferred a boy, naturally enough. I was the ultimate feminine girl, although nine and a half pounds. I was small boned and doll-like, my dark hair extremely thick and long, my skin a deep tan. The Welsh midwife called me Topsy, this was the name you gave to a black doll in those days. Always at school when she saw me she would fondle my hair and call me her Topsy. I suppose she must have delivered a great many Tenby babies and kept her fondness for them. Our next door neighbours at that time were Mr and Mrs Bye and their son Edwin. In those days when a new baby was born neighbours and friends called to see it. Edwin was intrigued with me and asked my mother what she meant to call me. Mother replied that she didn't know as it was another 'blooming' girl and she had wanted a boy. She must have been down to use Cockney rhyming slang, as I can never remember her doing so. Edwin said: "Why don't you call her Avis?" Which she did, I got Olwyn - Welsh for white clover - as my second name. I was christened in Saint Mary's Church, Mrs Lemon from the Maudlins was my Godmother.

Born with a vivid imagination, a mind eager to learn and quite good recall. I can remember back to being in the pram and playing with the tassel type knobs on the sideboard. My sister Joyce, whom by now you will have realised was more like a mother to me than my real mother, recalls what would happen when I was dressed up to be taken for a walk by two of the elder ones. They would sometimes wheel me around the Serpentine Road to Heywood Lane, then one would get in each side of me in the big pram and free-wheel down the steep hill to the Green. All who know Heywood Lane will wonder how I survived!

I often wonder if this is why I am so timid about doing things, I certainly never inherited my father's courage, but survive I did. As the baby in a big family you are in a favoured position for a short while. You sleep in your mother's bed as it is easier to feed a hungry baby this way. With five sisters to see to me, I didn't want for attention and played the part of the baby in their games. The things I learned from my elder sisters put me in a forward position when I started school aged four.

On October 30th 1937 my mother gave birth to a son at last, nine and a half pounds in weight. Alan Victor - she must have had Alan in mind for his name for some years and Victor was after a favourite brother of hers. Although only two, I can remember the night of his birth. I was taken out of my mother's bed and put in the big cot in the front room, the door of which was left open and the light on the stairs was filtering through the bars of the cot. I didn't like it. I knew something frightening was happening. After delivering a prefect baby boy, the midwife looked in to see me her Topsy. She said, "You mustn't cry, you've got a lovely baby brother." I said to take him back in that black bag, I want to be the baby ... which caused her to laugh as she bumped downstairs.

In fact, I cannot remember feeling jealous of my brother - love, sympathy and compassion were my emotions not jealousy. It was not easy to be a boy among six girls, as you can imagine. He fought for his manliness, when they tried to dress him up, to play with him as a doll. I can remember him at my mother's breast, little face red with crying. She had fed all of us and was proud of the fact, but after so many babies I don't think she had the milk for Alan. She was always trying and he was always crying. She soon pronounced him more trouble than all the girls put together.

He was her last child. To some extent he was my little playmate until I started school. He loved our spaniel Prince and we played in the garden, but as soon as he was old enough to feel his feet he was off barefoot to the woods. Catching rabbits like a little wild gypsy boy. He was friends with two brothers across the road, John and Tony Pilson, they had such kind parents and gave us such a lot of love. We will never forget them.

FERMANAGH RESCUE

Alan was three months old, when our father was to take part in one of Tenby Lifeboat's most memorable rescues. I have to quote the details as I was only two myself.

In the early hours of January 15th 1938 the phone rang for dad. The Coastguards informed him that the Lifeboat was on call-out, distress flares had been sighted out to sea off Saint Catherine's Island.

My father's sea clothes were always laid in readiness on the floor beside the bed, his size nine boots with thick white socks placed ready for his feet to slide into. It must be a mile or more from Broadwell Hayes to the Castle Hill and the Lifeboat Station. He had to cycle as fast as he could against a very strong wind and driving rain. Down the Maudlins, across the Green, up Saint John's Hill [nowadays a one-way street in the opposite direction] across the Norton and down Crackwell Street [again nowadays one-way] to the Lifeboat Station.

The conditions this morning were so bad ... he had to crawl on his hands and knees to get across the foot-bridge linking the Lifeboat Station to the Castle Hill, clinging to the wooden slats or he would have been blown away. Hurricane force winds and torrential rain. The sea was so rough ... it was breaking over the Napoleonic fortress on Saint Catherine's Island.

At 05:15 am within minutes of the first call the Tenby Lifeboat, of name *John R Webb II*, was launched on her fearful mission. Her crew anticipating a dangerous rescue, darkness and extreme weather conditions against them. Her Coxswain George Hooper was away at the time, his place taken by Second Coxswain John Rees.

Just handling the Lifeboat was a feat in itself in the severe conditions. Visibility was very poor due to the driving rain and spray from the waves. When they sighted the stricken ship they found her aground on the treacherous Woolhouse Rocks - which lie between Caldey Island and the mainland and are submerged at high water. She was identified as a coaster, the *SS Fermanagh* of Belfast.

The Lifeboat went into rescue procedure. Firstly to circle the ship, inspecting her position, checking for damage and searching for anyone in the water - priority always being given to these first. The ship seemed to be lying on an even keel and did not show signs of breaking up. The Coxswain decided it would be best to stand by and wait for better light, keeping a careful watch on any change in her position.

Within a short time of this decision the *Fermanagh* came off the rocks and was drifting before the gale. Her bows were up in the air and her decks awash two thirds of the way aft to her funnel and bridge. The Lifeboat crew could now see men aboard her.

The Acting Coxswain, John Rees, at once took the Lifeboat alongside her, handling his craft with great skill in the heavy seas, even so she could only stay alongside for a few seconds. In that short time the eight man crew of the *Fermanagh* were aboard the Lifeboat. My father told us that in order to exercise this feat the crew had to hook their feet in the scuppers and lean out with their arms outstretched, ready to grab any man who might not succeed in the jump.

FERMANAGH RESCUE 23

It was then discovered that her Master was not among them. Before the Lifeboat had arrived he had launched the ship's boat, but with the heavy seas he had been swept away.

The Lifeboat had already searched around the *Fermanagh* as she lay on the rocks and seen nothing of the Master or the ship's boat. The rescued men were in a state of shock and exhaustion. The Lifeboat headed for Tenby arriving at 08:30 am - just three hours and fifteen minutes from launch. They landed the rescued men and then went back to search for the Master. They searched for a further two hours but could find no trace of him. The Lifeboat returned to Tenby at 10:45 am, she had been out for over five hours and her crew were severely shaken in the heavy seas. They had been in continual danger of being washed overboard, and two of them were nearly lost when the Lifeboat went into a deep trough.

The highest praise possible must go to any man prepared to offer his life to save that of another.

The crew were: Second Coxswain, Acting Coxswain, John Rees - awarded the RNLI's Silver Medal; Mechanic Alfred Cottam - awarded the RNLI's Bronze Medal; the rest of the crew - all Tenby men, they were from old Lifeboat families - Fred Harries, Thomas E Lewis, Frank Hooper, Alexander Harries, Bertie Lewis, Henry Thomas and James N Crockford - were awarded Vellum Certificates for Gallantry from the RNLI.

Out of the blue as you might say, Eric Bancroft, Honorary Secretary of Tenby RNLI 1980-94 and now Honorary President (no nicer man has ever lived) was to encounter literature from one of the Fermanagh crew, John Macarthur the First Mate, of which he so kindly sent me copies. A marvellous man was the late John Macarthur, he died February 15th 1992. I will relate his story now as it gives completion to the rescue.

24 A TENBY LIFEBOAT FAMILY

John Macarthur first wrote to the RNLI two weeks after the rescue on February 3rd 1938, expressing thanks on behalf of the crew, and thanking the Tenby Lifeboat for their bravery and endurance.

Forty-nine years later [1987] he wrote again. His son Alistair, now a grown man had come to Tenby on holiday and visited the Lifeboat Station to give thanks as he felt he too owed them his life. His father John had not mentioned the rescue to his two sons as they were growing up to any great detail. But as a man Alistair had asked him for more detailed information. He couldn't have asked a more able man to write, relate and draw from memory the crew's side of things.

John was of retirement age when he wrote, but his recall was fantastic. His wife had ill health and although he had always wished to return to Tenby he had been unable to do so. His story of the events are in *italics* as follows:

The SS Fermanagh of Belfast left Drogheda [on the east coast of Ireland to the north of Dublin] on Thursday 13th January 1938 en route for Llanelli, South Wales, to load coal for Dundalk [north of Drogheda]. The weather was not too bad until the evening of the 14th when we missed the tide into Llanelli.

We then proceeded [across Carmarthen Bay] to Man-o-War Roads off Caldey Island to await the next tide. As the weather was getting worse we hove up anchor and proceeded towards Llanelli. On approach the Skipper considered it more prudent to return to Man-o-War Roads for shelter, pending improvement in the weather, which we did. But the weather showed no mercy and by 01:00 am on Saturday 15th January the wind was gusting to hurricane force.

All of a sudden the port anchor snapped and the remaining starboard anchor started dragging. We tried very hard to heave it aboard but failed to do so as the stud linked cable had apparently stretched and the gypsy segments on the anchor windlass wouldn't grip the cable. Time and again we tried and it kept slipping off. We endeavoured to slip the anchor's cable free of the ship with a view of making a run for it up the Bristol Channel, but this also proved impossible. I can't remember how long we were involved in this operation.

Whilst we were discussing the dilemma with the Skipper, Captain Hoy, we first felt a bump from the Woolhouse Rocks on the hull, for a moment we seemed to be stationary then the ship lurched heavily to starboard. The waves had pushed us so that we virtually slid off the rocks. The Skipper sent me down to the engine-room and to report back to him what the situation was below. The Chief Engineer told me everything seemed okay.

I then went back to the Skipper and whilst reporting to him the bridge telegraph was rung vigorously. I returned immediately to the engine-room where the Chief Engineer reported that the water was rising from the engine-room's bilge and was showing in the main engine's crankpit. I returned back to the Skipper and told him. He then sent me back to the Chief Engineer to tell him to close all valves and to open the boiler's blow-down cock to avoid the possibility of the boiler exploding, and then for all below in the engine-room and stockhold to come up on deck.

By the time the Chief Engineer came up on deck he reported that the water was up to the second step of the stair ladder from the engine-room. Until the water level in the engine-room and stockhold equalised with the external water level, it literally poured in and the ship steadily settled down by the stern. We had sent up distress rockets but at that time we had no idea if they had been seen.

The Skipper then decided to endeavour to launch the Fermanagh's starboard lifeboat, which in view of the prevailing weather conditions seemed to offer the best choice. After some effort we succeeded in swinging the boat out on its davits. No sooner had we managed to lower the boat down into the sea when we were hit with a succession of large waves, probably three in number. The net result was we lost the Skipper and the ship's boat.

Just after this happened we saw the red and green lights of what we assumed was the RNLI riding towards us. From the direction she came we formed the impression that she had surfed over the Woolhouse Rocks in order to approach us. This was discussed by us later on Sunday when we were travelling home, we agreed that this was so. It was a great feat of seamanship.

When we spotted the red and green lights of the Lifeboat a couple of blankets were soaked in paraffin and ignited. Charlie Spence, one of the stokers, was burned about the arms during this operation. It was to let the Lifeboat crew know that we were still on the Fermanagh.

The Lifeboat made several trial approaches, and then stood by maintaining a position of about 150 to 200 yards astern. Apparently awaiting dawn, and yet in strategic position if emergency action was required sooner.

The Fermanagh must have, with her bows high in the air, been travelling with some degree of forward movement in the direction of wind and sea, since the Lifeboat seemed to maintain her position - due to bows up the ship was acting as a balloon jib, whilst wind pressure on funnel and bridge structure had some stabilising effect she was continually yawing from side to side.

With the first brightening of dawn we saw the Lifeboat riding towards us. Fine on the stern starboard quarter. Then when close, they came surfing on the top of a big wave. The high degree of skill and co-ordination between the Coxswain and the Motor Mechanic holding her on the top of the wave, at the same time bringing her as close as two feet off our hull.

Our assembly point was close to the funnel, on the superstructure behind the bridge. Whilst we all jumped together, in a matter of seconds. As soon as we jumped the crew grabbed us and whipped us below into the after cockpit.

The Lifeboat that picked us up also had a forward cockpit with rudder shafting connecting through to the after or main cockpit, so that she could be steered from the bows. In that type of operational rescue its versatility was of some advantage.

When the crew got us below we were all given a good tot of spirits. It was only after that that I noticed we were all soaking wet. I had a pair of three-quarter length boots on, they were full of seawater and I hadn't noticed it before.

We told the Coxswain about losing the Skipper and the ship's boat and approximately the direction we had seen his torch signalling, and then lost sight of it. He said, "We'll land you first and go out again to search for him."

We were landed at the harbour in Tenby about 08:30 on the Saturday morning and the Lifeboat immediately turned and went to sea again.

I have always thought that Captain Hoy must have seen the red and green lights of the Lifeboat coming before we did and was possibly trying to attract their attention with his pocket torch. But I doubt from the angle the Lifeboat came from, that they had the remotest chance of seeing his flashing light, such were the severe conditions prevailing that morning.

The people of Tenby looked after us very well, indeed we were treated like Royalty. It is almost fifty years since then, but the fragrance of the memory is still as fresh even now as I write these words.

At times the wind was so severe, if you faced it, you couldn't get your breath. You had to turn your head to carry on breathing.

The British Isles, at that weekend, was lashed with severe gales and havoc was widespread amongst the shipping. There were many casualties. Tides were exceptionally high. Belfast had a tide five feet in height above normal.

28 A TENBY LIFEBOAT FAMILY

One of our company's ships, the SS Montalto, had to heave to off the Smalls Lighthouse [some twenty miles out to sea off the Pembrokeshire Coast]. With one of her two lifeboats washed overboard, the other badly damaged, most of her bridge washed away, together with her compasses. Her skipper Johnny Blair gradually worked her towards the Tusker Rock Lighthouse off the south-east coast of Ireland. She was brought into Belfast late on Sunday night the 16th January where she had to undergo major repairs. She had come from London loaded with a cargo of cement for Glasgow. This was a marvellous piece of seamanship in itself.

On the same night the Captain and First Officer of the Liverpool steamer the SS Suffolk Coast were washed overboard, off the Pembrokeshire coast, when her bridge and wheelhouse were washed away - a seaman off her was injured and was brought ashore by the Angle Lifeboat for treatment. The Welsh ship SS Glanrhyd was lost off the Gower coast, I believe all the crew were lost.

As I mentioned earlier I had not related this experience to my sons in any detail. As seafaring was not a popular subject with my wife, her father and only brother were lost at sea in the Atlantic, due to enemy action in the 1939-45 War. I myself had taken part in the Dunkirk Evacuation from France in the SS Saintfield.

The final ironic twist of the knife in my being rescued on this fateful night only became apparent three days after I arrived home. The news came through that the same storm that I had survived had claimed my brother Sam. Whose ship that had sailed from Waterford, Eire, bound for Swansea was missing with all hands lost. These are my thoughts ...

The sea still keeps its own secret
And the gift of life exacts its own price
Whilst we who are left still mourn

Of all the voluntary organisations I regard the RNLI as perhaps the most unique, in its character and especially its personnel, still performing its original function as laid down by its founding fathers.

I was born on the 13th June 1906 and as a small boy played in and around the local Lifeboat launching slip. The propulsion then was oars and sails, I couldn't possibly have foreseen the changes that lay in the future.

I can remember seeing, in 1912, my first aeroplane. The advancement in air transport since that time is staggering, consider then the equally great changes in the field of RNLI equipment. Particularly in the propulsion, plus new designs of hulls and electronics, together with the additional 'right arm' of the helicopter. We have arrived at the marriage of airmanship and seamanship, what other aids lie in the future?

I envy a future generation who will be able to perceive the RNLI still fulfilling the precepts and aims of the founding fathers.

*There were eight of us rescued by RNLI **John R Webb II**, of Tenby, and I now 81 years of age am probably the sole remaining survivor. The Fermanagh sank fifteen minutes after the completion of rescue. I had to make a sketch in order to awaken my memory. I have lost some sleep during the night hours trying to get the details sorted before writing to you. On that particular night, due to the conditions it was difficult to be what I would call orientated.*

*The crew of **John R Webb II** performed the type of seaworthy skill that one might see only once in a lifetime, and I am indeed privileged to have that remembrance.*

I trust I have not been too long-winded, I can only plead in mitigation that of all the talents, eloquence is the only one that does not reach its full strength until 'old age.'

I wish this inclusion to my family story to be a tribute to John Macarthur and his family who kindly agreed to me using his written work. As well as to the members of the Tenby Lifeboat who made this memorable rescue possible.

However old we are, we never understand life, with all its beauty and cruelty. It is important for us living to pass on the experience of our betters. In the hope that they will set an example for the young generation to follow. They were all heroes of their time and it was history on our own shores in the making. Fortunately, we don't encounter these extreme conditions often.

It seems the bad weather continued for some time and prevented the crew from returning the Lifeboat to the Lifeboat Station until four o'clock in the afternoon.

Even then however tired they may be, the ship has to be put in order. Every detail as it should be - ready for the next call-out. Had it been the same day, these men would still have gone out, assuming they were fit enough and, if not, a reserve would quickly be found.

For my father there was no such thing as a day off. It was a seven day a week job, on call twenty-four hours a day. So your family life had its limitations. He did sometimes go to the Royal Playhouse Cinema - where he sat in a special seat, so they knew where to find him and the Coastguards would have been previously informed.

I follow with a verse of tribute to the Tenby Lifeboat.

*(Publisher's note: This chapter, **Tenby Lifeboat Heroes** and **Happy Reunions** have been reviewed by the Coxswain of Tenby Lifeboat Alan Thomas. My mother, Nesta (née Rowse) Fish, can remember as a young woman seeing the survivors of the **Fermanagh Rescue** in Tenby Post Office sending off telegrams to their loved ones and families to inform them of their rescue and safety. (The post office was then situated in Tudor Square with a panoramic view overlooking Tenby Harbour and Carmarthen Bay from the serving counter.) Further examples of the author's poetry can be found on the Internet in the **Star of Pembrokeshire Poetry Anthology** which is accessible from the publisher's homepage.)*

LIFEBOATMAN POEM

The Lifeboatman
A tribute to the Tenby Lifeboat by
Avis Nixon (née Cottam)

The Lifeboat launches
From the Slip
To try to save
The sinking ship
Do haste all men
Your help they need

You work through God
To answer prayer
Through every storm
You must be brave
Your fellow men
You must save

Who chose this role
For you to play
It is not any
Thought of pay
But in your heart
You bear a pride
Something deep
Down inside

That lesser men
Could never know
On Stock Exchange
Or Saville Row
One life we have
To live or give
Some may be loath
The Lifeboatman
Does both.

TENBY LIFEBOAT HEROES

*(Publisher's note: As referenced on pages 2 & 6 the author would like to express her gratitude to **Jeff Morris** for allowing her to use his illustrated book **Tenby Lifeboats** as the foundation research for this chapter. The author would also like to recognise the help with her researches of Tenby RNLI and its Honorary Secretary Arthur Squibbs.*

Mr Morris' book, which covers the period to 1986, is obtainable from Tenby RNLI by mail-order at £1.50 (incl. p&p worldwide by surface mail) with cheques made payable to Tenby RNLI (c/o DLA Wyn Griffiths, Hafod-Y-Coed, Seascape, Tenby, Pembrokeshire, SA70 8JL).

*Further copies of **A Tenby Lifeboat Family** and other titles in the **Star of Pembrokeshire** series (refer to pages 4 & 5) can likewise be obtained by mail-order for £12.50 from Tenby RNLI.*

*Also available is a CD entitled **The Tenby Lifeboatman** by local musicians **The Bushwackers** at £5; includes tracks entitled 'The Tenby Lifeboatman,' 'The Caldey Boatman's Song' and 'When The Tide Comes In.'*

*All profits from Tenby RNLI retailing going to the fund for the proposed new Tenby Lifeboat Station and new Tenby Lifeboat (refer to the first chapter **Sacred Ground**).*

Living in a town as beautiful as Tenby, humble mortals such as we have a lot to live up to. It instils a pride in us and aspires us to do it justice in our actions.

It doesn't matter to some extent if our deeds are small and unnoticed. What matters is that we feel we have made a contribution.

Man is born to conquer and create in order to live and improve his life. In every generation certain men are born to be greater than others. Such a man, in our era in Tenby, was **Charles Ivor Crockford**.

Born in 1912 to a family with a long seafaring history, he was one of five sons born to Mr and Mrs James Rolfe

Crockford. Christened Charles Ivor, he was always called Ivor. His life's interest was to be the sea.

He followed in the family tradition of Lifeboat Service, and joined the crew of the Tenby Lifeboat in 1938 as Signalman. He was twenty-six years old. My father had been Mechanic there for five years at this time. Ivor went on to become Bowman, Second Coxswain and finally Coxswain. He had spent his early years in the Merchant Navy and served in the Royal Naval Reserve.

One year after his joining the Tenby Lifeboat, it was 1939 and the outbreak of the Second World War, Ivor joined the Royal Navy. He was a young man of twenty-seven who already had years of seamanship to his credit. He was to go forth and serve his country in their time of need.

My father was exempt from this War Service because of his position as Lifeboat Mechanic.

During the War, Ivor saw Active Service and was commissioned in 1942. He took part in the memorable Dunkirk Evacuation and in the hazardous Normandy Landings when he commanded a tank-landing craft.

Right at the front line of battle, he served in the English Channel on motor torpedo boats. His bravery in this Service earned him a mention in 'dispatches.' So much one is called on to give for one's country in the time of War, for so little. I wanted as far as possible to praise our **Tenby Lifeboat Heroes**. It is only thanks to the written and spoken word that we are able to do so.

Any one of his valiant deeds was something a man fighting for his country could be proud of.

With Ivor it seemed wherever there was crucial action so was he. Plucked by fate to be at the helm. Chosen by the God he served.

The end of the War and one might think Ivor had seen enough of the sea and its hazards. But no, he was raring to go to sea. Anywhere in the world. Now in his late thirties and through the 1950s, he made a number of winter cruises

34 A TENBY LIFEBOAT FAMILY

to South Africa as quartermaster on the old Union Castle shipping line's *Caernarvon Castle*.

Back to Tenby now, but none the less enterprising, he was for many years one of our best known pleasure boat operators and introduced larger vessels to Tenby Harbour's fleet, despite opposition. The first of these was the *Saucy Sue* with a passenger load of forty-eight, and later the *Enterprise* which carried a hundred passengers.

In 1970 at the age of fifty-eight, he began a new venture, operating the motor vessel *Tudor Prince* from Hobbs' Point, Pembroke Dock, on cruises up the Milford Haven Waterway and the River Daugleddau.

I had a shop in Milford Haven at this time and I can remember this venture starting. It opened up a very beautiful river to many who had never seen it before, including locals.

The *Tudor Prince* was the largest pleasure cruiser in Pembrokeshire carrying one hundred and fifty passengers. Who else would be at the helm but Ivor?

Just two years prior to this, on one notable occasion on November 14th 1968, Ivor, then Second Coxswain on the Tenby Lifeboat **Henry Comber Brown**, was at home convalescing after being in hospital for some time. But when the maroons went off, he rose and rushed to the Lifeboat to take command as he knew the Coxswain, William Thomas, was suffering ill health and was due to retire after forty-three years with the Tenby Lifeboat crew.

The Motor Mechanic, Leslie Day, had just retired after serving sixteen years service with the Tenby Lifeboat, eleven and a half of them as Mechanic. So Assistant Mechanic Raymond Thomas and Emergency Mechanic Brian Bolton, took his place and the Lifeboat was launched with a full crew.

In very heavy seas she battled her way to the stricken vessel *MV Manta*. The coaster's gears had broken down and the Lifeboat stood by while a tug took her in tow. They then escorted both vessels into Milford Haven.

The seas were too heavy at Tenby to allow the Lifeboat to be rehoused in the Lifeboat Station, so she moored at Pembroke Dock until she could return two days later.

Ivor Crockford's doctor later wrote that his action to this duty must have taken immense courage, with complete disregard for considerable pain and discomfort. After this he became Coxswain. James Bulley became Mechanic.

For his dedication to the Lifeboat Service, Ivor Crockford received a framed Letter of Thanks, signed by the Chairman of the RNLI Admiral Sir Wilfred Woods GBE. Assistant Mechanic Raymond Thomas also received a Letter of Thanks.

A true Christian, he devoted a great deal of his leisure time to the Tenby Charity Trustees, an organisation which administers funds acquired over the years from benefactors for the elderly and needy of the town.

His heart and loyalty towards his seaside home got him involved with local politics where he would lend his personality and strength to aid his fellow men.

He was elected to Tenby Borough Council, and during his eighteen years with this authority, he was elected as Alderman, served as a Deputy Mayor and had two terms of office as Mayor.

Never lordly. Versatile and friendly he gave his support to many of the town's activities: Tenby Rugby Club, Sea Cadets, Tenby Harbour Users' Association. He was a former President of the Chamber of Trade, a founder member of the Royal Naval Association and had early association with the Tenby Sailing Club.

Land or sea, wherever a ship needed steering, there was our worthy Ivor.

No intention of being inactive after retirement, he devoted a great deal of his leisure time and interest into helping at the Tenby Museum and Art Gallery on Castle Hill where he welcomed thousands of visitors with his affable charm and gave them the very essence of Tenby.

36 A TENBY LIFEBOAT FAMILY

In my father's time with the Tenby Lifeboat, *John R Webb II* had been at the station for three years when dad was appointed Mechanic. He served until 1948. The *John R Webb II* continued in commission until 1955.

The new Lifeboat *Henry Comber Brown* was to be in service in Tenby for over thirty years. The Annual Lifeboat Service of 1986 was to be a colourful Service of Thanksgiving, held on the Castle Hill on Sunday August 1st, to say a sad and fond farewell to this notable vessel.

She was especially launched for the occasion and took centre position in the bay between the congregation on the Castle Hill and the fortress on Saint Catherine's Island. Very moving. The Rector of Tenby, Archdeacon Dewi Bridges, officiated the Service. The lessons were read by the Chairman of the RNLI Management Committee Mr Jack Thomas and Tenby Councillor Mickey Folland. The hymns rang out over the beloved vessel and resounded on the rocks and caves of the island. What a fitting tribute for a ship that had helped to save so many lives.

I would like to end this tribute to this fine man, Charles Ivor Crockford, with an extract [page 41] from some of his own reminiscences as it typifies his personality and the manner in which he conducted his life.

No lowly position was too low for him, and no command too high. In this alone, he was a great man.

I quote from Tenby RNLI records: *"As the **Henry Comber Brown** leaves her service in Tenby, several former members of the crew were looking back on the times they manned her and the tales they had to tell, including a well-known former Coxswain Ivor Crockford, who was on board her for her sea trials and initial voyage to Tenby."*

Like the *Henry Comber Brown* herself, Ivor had actively served with the Tenby Lifeboat crew for over thirty years; serving with his father, brother, two sons and seven nephews - who now carry on the family's Lifeboat tradition in Tenby.

Ivor remembered that during the 1955 trials, he held the important position of Cook, being responsible for providing three square meals for the crew, despite a bout of seasickness on board.

His first impression of the boat was that she threw a lot of sea aboard in bad weather.

On one occasion after escorting a vessel for ten hours they put into Minehead on the Bristol Channel, Somerset. A hotel was opened up for them providing hot meals and baths. Tommy 'Dowie' Howells fell asleep in the bath, fully clothed. They were so exhausted.

Mr Leslie Day was also a long serving crew member as Mechanic under the command of Coxswains Tommy 'Josh' Richards and Billy 'Ila' Thomas. Leslie Day recalled that on one occasion he was locked in the engine-room by Josh and ordered to fix the injector pump. As a reward for his repairs he was allowed the first cup full from the rum bottle.

Leslie Day added that if you knew the *Henry Comber Brown* you could always get her to her destination, whatever the trouble.

Eternal as the sea. These men will never die.

A Lifeboatman for forty-five years and a true 'Son of the Sea' was **George Henry Hooper**. He died at the age of seventy-eight in 1957.

Born in Tenby in 1879 he was one of eleven children from the late Mr and Mrs Robert Hooper who came from Devonshire.

His father was the Skipper of one of the Brixham trawlers which fished from Tenby many years ago.

George himself was only nine years old when he first went to sea with his father in 1898, and he was to be a fisherman all his life, except when on War Service.

A member of the Royal Naval Reserve, he was called up before the outbreak of the First World War, when he would have been twenty-five years old, and he served throughout the hostilities for some five years.

He was referred to daily in our home because of serving with dad, and we always called him Mr Hooper. He was a highly respected man, but he did have a nickname: 'The Long 'Un.'

Mr Hooper joined the crew of the Tenby Lifeboat in 1911 when he was twenty-two years old. He was the Coxswain twenty-two years later when my father joined in 1933.

He was to take part in many of the early rescues, which must have been hard and hazardous, depending on the muscle power of the oarsmen. Their endurance is beyond our comprehension.

The *William and Mary Devey* was placed at the Tenby Lifeboat Station in November 1902. When George Hooper joined the crew she had been there for nine years. She was a 38 foot by 9 foot 4 inches, 12 oared, non-self-righting Watson class; designed for sailing greater distances than the smaller self-righting boats. She cost £984 to build and the old Boathouse had to be altered to accommodate her at a cost of £289. Built in 1894 the old Boathouse still exists, next to the Castle Sands slipway, as does the original Boathouse [1852] on the Quay Sands next to the Harbour wall.

Her Coxswain, **Thomas Davies**, retired at the end of 1911, and was succeeded by **John Williams**. Mr George Hooper was a member of his crew. This rowing Lifeboat took part in many rescues.

At three in the afternoon of Boxing Day 1912, the French schooner *Marie Emilie Andrea* of Lorient, which had been dragging her anchors for some time, got into a very dangerous position and her crew signalled for help.

The Lifeboat was launched at 15:15 and battled through very heavy seas, whipped by a westerly gale. On reaching the casualty the Lifeboat stood by for some time, but as the seas grew steadily worse it was decided to take the crew off the schooner.

TENBY LIFEBOAT HEROES

The six men were successfully taken aboard the Lifeboat which brought them back to Tenby, but such considerable difficulty was experienced getting her into harbour in the violent seas that several oars were broken as the crew struggled to bring the Lifeboat alongside the quay.

No praise is too high for these veteran Lifeboatmen who fulfilled their role with strength and courage and little else.

Tenby and Caldey Island are of course inseparable, and another rescue, in which Mr Hooper and the crew of the *William and Mary Devey* took part was two months later on February 18th 1913.

The ketch *Cornish Lass of Plymouth* owned by the Reverend Father Abbot of Caldey and used as a supply vessel for the monastery, got into difficulties west of Caldey Island in an easterly gale.

The *William and Mary Devey* was launched at 10 pm. It was a dark night, but they quickly reached the ketch and took off the crew of three. On her way back to Tenby, the Lifeboat encountered mountainous seas and she was forced to shelter in the lee of the Royal Victoria Pier [built in 1899 and demolished in 1953, now the proposed site of a new Lifeboat House and Slip referred to in the **Sacred Ground** opening chapter] until 01:15 am when the weather eased sufficiently for her to get into the harbour.

These men had then been at sea for over three hours in tremendous seas, and the cold and dark of a February night, and they still had to use their hands and limbs to fulfil their rescue.

The Lifeboat crew of Tenby have always been a united and affectionate family. It is impossible too write about one without the other, and I certainly have no wish to do so, as I feel the love for their fellow men and their joint ambition is a characteristic to be very proud of as is their devotion and bravery.

40 A TENBY LIFEBOAT FAMILY

I feel very privileged, as a Lifeboatman's daughter to be able to relate these tales to you. Some of you, like myself, were brought up on them, so to speak. But for many others, who may read them for the first time in this family story, I hope they will appreciate the quality of the town through the character of its people as well as its natural beauty. In today's society, Tenby is quite unique.

None of this side of my work would have been possible without the help of the Tenby Lifeboat personnel, and the kind help of the Tenby Museum and Art Gallery. All has been unselfishly given. I shall endeavour to repay this debt of gratitude throughout the rest of my life. I am indebted to Tenby Lifeboats by Jeff Morris, for his fine work.

I have been honoured by having a copy of my book placed in the Tenby Museum and Art Gallery for the future reference of the town, and the Haverfordwest Public Library for student reference. So I am already very proud.

I include the following story in my tribute to my father's Coxswain, George Henry Hooper, although it is related to some extent by our former hero, Ivor Crockford, as it refers to Mr Hooper's father and family, and Ivor was a boy at the time of this rescue.

On the January 16th 1987, former Coxswain Ivor Crockford related an old tale about the Tenby Lifeboat in the days of canvas. He had been reading through the old records kept by the late Dr E M R Bryant of Saint Julian's Street, Tenby, who was Honorary Secretary of Tenby Lifeboat Station from 1900 to 1929.

I quote: *"On the night of December 1st 1919 a ketch was seen to be driving ashore on the South Sands, near the Iron Bar which is under the Paragon. The Coxswain J 'Naff' Williams, who saw her come ashore, immediately fired the maroons and launched the Tenby Lifeboat **William and Mary Devey**."*

TENBY LIFEBOAT HEROES 41

The Rocket Lifesaving Team [breeches-buoy] were also called and arrived first at the scene of the wreck. This is the Coxswain J 'Naff' Williams' report:

Name: *Venguri of Groix, France. Lightship bound for Port Talbot.*
Rig of wreck: *Ketch, 48 tons.*
State of sea: *Heavy gale – heaving ground sea and heavy rain.*
Wreck first sighted: *8:50 pm.*
Lifeboat slipped: *9 pm.*
Reached wreck: *9:45 pm under canvas and oars.*
Picked out: *Crew of four men and a boy.*
Returned to harbour: *10:45 pm.*
Lifeboat rehoused: *10 am the following day.*
Coxswain's note: *Service carried out under sail and oars. Boat behaved well – no damage – one oar broken – anchor rope cut – grapnel and lifelines parted. The Rocket Lifesavers got a Rocket Line across, but the crew of the stricken vessel were done in and seemed confused. Jimmy Folland fired the shot first time, but the breeches-buoy was not secured. So we went alongside, took off four men and a boy of twelve – then buggered off!*

The Crew on this rescue were: Coxswain J 'Naff' Williams, Second Coxswain Robert Hooper (father of George and Charlie) Bowman John 'Jack Skeep' Rees (Mrs Flo Eynon's father) James Davies (Jack Davies' grandfather) J Williams (of San Domingo) George 'The Long 'Un' Hooper, Jim Crockford (Ivor Crockford's father) Josh Richards (Peter Richards' grandfather) Fred Goodridge, Harry Hooper (Lesley Hooper's father) Tom Kingdom, John Rees (Nelson Rees' father) Henry 'Dubs' Thomas, William Thomas (Mrs Child's father and grandfather to the present Coxswain Alan Thomas).

Mr Ivor Crockford added his personal memories of this old sea rescue. I quote: *"I remember this rescue very well. I was eight years old and one of dozens of locals watching the*

42 A TENBY LIFEBOAT FAMILY

rescue at the Iron Bar end. Others included on this night were Lal John, Billy 'Ila,' Billy Smith, Jack 'Sprat,' 'Nantal' Phillips, Albert Marsh, Billy 'Dubs,' Reg Stacey, Vic Rees, Flanagan and Dinky Crockford.

"The number one in the Rocket Crew was Mr Jim Folland. The first shot went right between the spars. Perfect. There appeared to be some confusion on board as the line was not secured. The Rocket Crew was unable to secure the breeches-buoy.

"Then the Lifeboat appeared under sail amid great roars from the crowd. She approached the wreck in a heavy and confused sea and belting rain.

"Came up head to wind, dropped the canvas and anchor and veered stern first alongside the vessel.

"She took off four men and a boy, hoisted the sail, hove in anchor, then cut it to save time.

"She then made for the harbour. A wonderful display of seamanship.

"A few days later, the vessel which had not been holed was patched up and brought into harbour. She lay alongside for four or five weeks, mending her sails and seeing to the hull.

"We made friends with the cabin boy, who was twelve. We nicknamed him 'Mush' and used to take him around the Castle Hill, collecting snails and cliff 'cabbage.'

"We were very sad when the crew eventually left for Port Talbot."

The **William and Mary Devey** finished her service in 1923. She was the last of the old sailing and rowing Lifeboats in Tenby and went out with a fine record of having been launched forty-six times in her twenty-one year's service.

She and her crew had saved seventy-nine lives, which proved to be the largest number of lives saved by any pulling and sailing Lifeboat on the south-west coast.

The first motor Lifeboat **John R Webb** arrived at the Tenby Lifeboat Station in August 1923.

George Hooper and the rest of the crew found themselves with a very different boat: 7 foot longer, 3 foot wider, nearly 3 times heavier. She had a six-cylinder petrol engine, her speed of eight and a half knots meant she was much faster. They had to adapt themselves to the new skills required to handle her in this new method of rescue. Also, modifications to the Boathouse and Slip, built in 1905, had to be made.

She was only stationed at Tenby for seven years. During that period she was launched sixteen times and she and her crew saved thirty-two lives. Her last service was in June 1928 and she remained at Tenby until 1930. On one occasion during a launch she was struck by lightning, but fortunately none of the crew were injured.

1930 now, and the *John R Webb II* was placed on service in Tenby. The same size as her predecessor and from the same donor, the legacy of Mr J R Webb of Leicester.

My father didn't know at this time but this Lifeboat was to be his life and nearly his death, for some fifteen years, as it was for Mr George Hooper.

George Hooper became her Coxswain in 1931 when the Coxswain John Williams retired - he had served as Coxswain of the Tenby Lifeboat for nineteen years, originally with the **William and Mary Devey** in 1912.

My father, Alfred Cottam, joined Mr Hooper as Motor Mechanic in 1933, when the Mechanic Arthur Ridley retired.

Together with their crew they were to take part in many rescues. Just a year later it was the famous **Fermanagh Rescue**, related in chapter four. George Hooper was unable to attend this rescue and his place was taken by the Second Coxswain John Rees, who received the RNLI's Silver Medal. My father received the Bronze Medal.

On one notable rescue they were both injured, as were other crew members, when the Lifeboat nearly capsized.

Midday on February 8th 1945, the Tenby Lifeboat Station had a call from Trinity House, Swansea, requesting that the

Lifeboat be sent to the Saint Govan's Lightship. The head-keeper was seriously ill and the lightship was short of stores.

The *John R Webb II* launched at 12:30 pm into a very rough sea, whipped up by a full south-westerly gale.

They had a long way to go to the lightship. Fifteen sea miles. And when they left the comparative shelter of Caldey Island, they met the full force of the violent storm.

High seas were repeatedly sweeping over the Lifeboat as she battled her way towards the lightship. They had travelled twelve miles in these conditions when suddenly an enormous wall of water broke right over her, smashing the steering wheel and bending the steering shaft.

Then another high wave crashed over the *John R Webb II* and nearly sank her. Her crew were now badly injured. The Coxswain, Second Coxswain, Mechanic (my father) and Second Mechanic, very badly.

On this rescue, our dear George Hooper was Acting Assistant Mechanic at the age of sixty-one years in order to make up a full crew. His injuries were serious. Several fractured ribs and a fractured pelvis. He must have been in considerable pain. My father was smashed about the head. He came home eventually, with his head swathed in white bandages. It affected his sight as he afterwards had to wear glasses and I can remember him sitting with his head in his hands, so great were the headaches.

I am sorry; I do not know how badly the other crew members were injured.

Despite being repeatedly swept by high waves, plus the injuries of the crew, the Lifeboatmen rigged up emergency steering and the battered Lifeboat and crew made their way back to Tenby.

A gallant attempt, but unable to fulfil this particular rescue.

When the storm eased somewhat the next day, the Angle Lifeboat went out to the lightship taking their requested stores and bringing the head-keeper ashore for treatment.

TENBY LIFEBOAT HEROES 45

George Hooper retired in 1945 and my father Alfred Cottam three years later in 1948.

In a Lifeboat crew each man is as brave as his fellow members. Interdependent, they are a united team. Each would take whatever position was required of them to fulfil their rescue. The most important person to them is the casualty.

This tribute to **Tenby Lifeboat Heroes** is to every one of our Lifeboatmen who have given their devoted service since 1852 when a Lifeboat Station was first founded in Tenby by the Shipwrecked Fishermen and Mariners' Benevolent Society - becoming part of the RNLI in 1854.

Those that I have portrayed were with my father and therefore part of my family story. My sincere thanks to all who made this possible. My sincere wish is that it will further the cause.

I find the illustrated book **Tenby Lifeboats** by **Jeff Morris**, on sale from Tenby RNLI [refer to start of chapter] and from Tenby bookshops, a very emotional experience and each time I read I cry ... and sometimes laugh at the local humour.

The bravery and self-sacrifice of our heroes has quietly passed by and but for the RNLI records and the written words by Jeff Morris would to a great extent be forgotten. I have endeavoured from these records to 'cameo our heroes.' My book has already achieved some notable success. I hope it will take the stories of their valour to further corners of the world and in so doing redress the balance of acclaim they are so worthy of, and further the cause of the Tenby Lifeboat and all who work so hard for her.

In 1946 **Thomas Benjamin Richards** succeeded Mr George Hooper as Coxswain and Len Beardmore succeeded my father, Alfred Cottam, as Motor Mechanic in 1948. My father had served for fifteen years and I don't really know the reason why he retired at this time. He was fifty-three years of age.

46 A TENBY LIFEBOAT FAMILY

Thomas Benjamin Richards was to be Coxswain, of first the ***John R Webb II*** and then the ***Henry Comber Brown***, for twelve years. The Richards' family have a long association with the Tenby Lifeboat, one generation after another. Well over one hundred years of service to the Tenby Lifeboat.

Thomas was a very brave and dutiful man. His devotion to the Tenby Lifeboat came second to none.

The following story from the book Tenby Lifeboats by Jeff Morris typifies his character:

On September 21st 1953, the ***John R Webb II*** took part in an outstanding rescue. That evening the Coastguard at Tenby learned that the pumps on the Saint Govan's Lightship had stopped working and she was in danger of sinking.

She had a crew of seven men on board. A full west-southwesterly gale was blowing and the sea was extremely rough, with a very heavy swell from the south-west, which was combining to cause an abnormally confused sea.

The District Officer of the Coastguard at Tenby later said: "I have experienced stronger winds during my service in Her Majesty's Coastguards, but I have never seen the sea so bad. This is the first time I had some hesitation in asking the Lifeboat to put to sea."

Within five minutes of the maroons being fired to call-out the crew, ***John R Webb II*** was launched. The time was 9:42 pm.

Once clear of Caldey Island, the Lifeboat was driving straight into the full fury of the storm. They had about fifteen miles to go.

The light vessel was without power and was only showing a small oil lantern in her rigging.

Coxswain Thomas Richards asked the lightship's Master by radio to fire flares at intervals to indicate her position, and shortly after at 12:30 am the Coxswain sighted one and the Lifeboat reached the light vessel at 1:10 am. Conditions were so appalling it had taken them three hours and twenty-eight minutes to travel the fifteen miles.

She was lying head to sea and wind, with the heavy swell on her port bow causing her to roll very heavily as the high seas swept over the lightship.

Her Master advised the Lifeboat Coxswain to approach on the starboard side.

Thomas Richards brought the Lifeboat alongside the heavy rolling lightship but in the violent seas and darkness the crew of the lightship were unable to make fast the securing rope, and as the high seas enveloped her, the *John R Webb II* was swept away.

A second run-in was made, and again, using his engines, Coxswain Richards held the Lifeboat alongside, with the aid of a rope from the lightship ... long enough for two men to be taken aboard the Lifeboat. The rope then parted and the Lifeboat was swept away for a second time.

A third run was made and again using his engines Coxswain Richards held the Lifeboat alongside. The Lifeboatmen lined their port rail and quickly hauled the remaining five men from the lightship, just as she rolled heavily on the Lifeboat causing some damage, but without injuring anyone.

Thomas Richards swung the bows of the *John R Webb II* away from the crippled lightship and headed back to Tenby arriving at 3:30 pm.

For his superb seamanship and outstanding courage, Thomas Benjamin Richards was awarded the Silver Medal by the RNLI, the Lifeboat's Bowman William Thomas and the Motor Mechanic William Rogers each received Bronze Medals. The other crew members each received Thanks on Vellum from the Institution. They are all our great **Tenby Lifeboat Heroes**.

Some of the call-outs are not great epics, but if their help is needed, out they go. They have to err on the side of caution.

William Ray Thomas succeeded Thomas Benjamin Richards as Coxswain of the Tenby Lifeboat *Henry Comber*

48 A TENBY LIFEBOAT FAMILY

Brown in 1958. During his ten years service as Coxswain, he and the Tenby Lifeboat crew were to go out to many rescues. One of which was to rescue pedigree cows that had fallen off the cliffs at Manorbier.

At Christmas they did their traditional launch to take parcels and provisions for the crews of the lightships nearby.

One very dramatic call-out was on the November 18th 1963. The coaster *Kilo* of 571 tons was on passage from Liverpool to Rotterdam carrying a lethal cargo of sodium, and in her hold she also had a cargo of whisky and acetone.

Minutes after her Master saw a small flame above a drum of sodium, the top of the drum was blown off by an explosion.

The vessel was east of the Smalls Lighthouse with a south-westerly gale force eight gusting to storm force ten. The Master decided to make for Swansea and put out a distress call. The ***Henry Comber Brown***, under the command of William Ray Thomas was launched at 12:50 am.

The *Kilo* was then in a position ten miles south-east of Caldey and the Coxswain planned to come up with her near the Helwick Lightship [off Worms' Head, Gower Peninsula].

At one stage the Lifeboat was laid on her beam-ends and the tarpaulin wheel-house doors were smashed off their rails (Barry Coastguards recorded a wind speed of 112 mph).

A Shackleton aircraft of coastal command was deployed to illuminate the coaster's position with parachute flares. Before the ***Henry Comber Brown*** could reach her, the Lifeboat's port engine lost oil pressure and had to be shut down.

The Mumbles Lifeboat was then launched and when she reached the casualty her Coxswain, Derek Scott, described *Kilo* as afire from stern to stem ... with the seas around her seemingly on fire as well. She eventually grounded and her crew were taken off by the Mumbles Lifeboat. Coxswain Scott was awarded the RNLI's Silver Medal.

TENBY LIFEBOAT HEROES 49

The Tenby Lifeboat continued on her course to Swansea. After battling through tremendous seas, on her starboard engine only, they entered South Dock just after eight am. They had been at sea for over seven hours.

The damage to her port engine was repaired and she returned to Tenby at 3:30 pm on Tuesday the 19th.

Sometimes some of the most difficult rescues happen quite close to home.

On the afternoon of August 27th 1966 the Coastguard reported that six people were trapped by the tide at the mouth of a cave near Waterwynch.

Although the Coastguard Cliff Rescue Team was reported to be on its way, Geoffrey Reason-Jones the Honorary Secretary of the Tenby Lifeboat Station knew, from past experience and his knowledge of the area, that it was likely that the Lifeboat would be needed. He hurried to the Lion Corner overlooking the north shore at Tenby and using his binoculars, he could see people trapped on some of the rocks. There was clearly a danger that they might be washed off before the Coastguards could reach them, so he decided to launch the Lifeboat.

Informing the Coastguards of his intentions, he headed for the Lifeboat Station and the maroons were fired. The *Henry Comber Brown* was launched at 4 pm taking a 14ft punt with her.

It was one hour before high water and although there was only a moderate sea there was a heavy swell from the southeast.

The Tenby Lifeboat dropped anchor off Waterwynch, only ten minutes after launching and Coxswain Thomas veered down towards the rocks.

Five boys could be seen huddled together on a narrow ledge and a girl was by herself on a rock nearby.

The Lifeboat got within seventy-five yards of the cliff face, but could not get any closer because of the heavy swell and some outcrops of rocks.

The Coxswain decided to use the punt, and Bowman Joshua Richards, and crew member Michael Wilson (a Second Officer in the Merchant Navy who was home on leave at this time) volunteered to man the punt.

Bowman Joshua Richards managed to work the punt within ten yards of the rocks. A considerable achievement requiring great skill and tremendous physical strength in the very heavy surf. The swell at times was fourteen feet high.

One boy dived into the sea and was hauled aboard the punt. He said that none of the others were good swimmers so, Michael Wilson secured a line to his life-jacket and while Joshua Richards struggled to keep the punt in position, the boy paid out the line.

Michael Wilson was completely lost from view in the high surf for most of his swim to the rocks. The surge of water, back off the cliff face, prevented him from climbing the ledge and so he persuaded one of the boys to jump into the sea and helped him to the punt. He returned three more times through the turmoil of broken water, and each time brought back one of the boys.

Bowman Joshua Richards then rowed back to the Lifeboat and the boys were put aboard.

Crew member Brian Bolton then joined his colleagues in the punt and they headed back for the rock on which the girl was stranded.

Michael Wilson again went into the sea but the girl, who could not swim, would not jump into the sea. Michael Wilson decided that the only way he was going to reach the girl was to allow himself to be literally washed up to the rocks by the waves. This he did, being badly bruised and cut in doing so. Once he'd recovered his breath he persuaded the girl to go back with him.

He tied the lifeline around her and they jumped into the sea and were hauled safely to the punt, which took them back to the Lifeboat and then to Tenby.

TENBY LIFEBOAT HEROES 51

For his act of truly outstanding personal bravery Michael Wilson was awarded the Silver Medal by the RNLI. For his considerable skill and gallantry, Bowman Joshua Richards was awarded the Bronze Medal. Michael Wilson later received the Maud Smith Award for the bravest act of lifesaving by a member of a Lifeboat in 1966.

Coxswain William Ray Thomas retired in 1968 because of ill health. Totally dedicated to the Tenby Lifeboat, he had served forty-three years. He was succeeded by Ivor Crockford.

The Richards' family have a long seafaring and Lifeboat history in Tenby. **Joshua William Richards**, son of the former Coxswain Thomas Benjamin Richards [1946-58] became Coxswain of the Tenby Lifeboat in 1972, succeeding Ivor Crockford - who had retired, thirty-four years from first joining the Tenby Lifeboat service in 1938.

Joshua Richards was to see an eventful first year as Coxswain. The *Henry Comber Brown* was fitted with a Decca 050 radar set and Tenby Lifeboat Station had its first inflatable Inshore Lifeboat (ILB) a fifteen-foot six-inch D-204 class powered by a 40 horsepower outboard engine with a top speed of 20 knots.

Just seven days after her arrival she was launched for the first time. Between that first service on July 16th 1972 and the end of August she was called-out fourteen times and saved ten lives. What an amazing start ... The following year she answered forty calls. A record!

Henry Comber Brown was launched thirty-two times that same year (1973) and these seventy-two call-outs were exactly the same number answered by the pulling and sailing boats over a 47 year period (1876-1923).

Besides the appointment of a new Coxswain and the introduction of the ILB (which being kept constantly busy had fully justified her role) 1972 marked the beginning of a period when other significant events were happening connected with the Tenby Lifeboat.

52 A TENBY LIFEBOAT FAMILY

In 1977 a new Boathouse [situated in Tenby Harbour at the top of the Mayor's Slip next to the Sluice] was opened for the ILB, having been built out of funds raised by the people of Tenby and district.

One rescue by the ILB on Friday August 26th 1977 at 4:02 pm was to rescue people cut off by the tide. D-204, which was her name, was launched after the Coastguard reported that a number of people were cut off by the tide beneath the Paragon on the South Sands, Tenby.

It was full flood tide with a choppy sea and heavy surf which made it difficult to approach the stranded people.

Four children and two adults were rescued and landed at Tenby Harbour. The Inshore Lifeboat then returned to the scene and rescued three more adults and a youth, landing them all at 5 pm. The rescue took an hour and saved ten lives.

Towards the end of 1978, during routine maintenance work on Tenby Lifeboat Station, engineers discovered extensive rot in the timber sub-structure. The ***Henry Comber Brown*** was placed on a mooring off Tenby Harbour and the Boathouse closed while further examination was carried out.

On January 2nd 1979, because of bad weather, the Coxswain Joshua Richards and crew took the ***Henry Comber Brown*** to a more sheltered mooring off Caldey Island. At ten o'clock the following morning they set off back to Tenby to change crew as there was still a force nine gale blowing with very heavy seas.

While the Lifeboat was lying alongside the harbour, Coxswain Richards learned that the five men who had spent the night on 'anchor watch' onboard the RAF pinnace [used to patrol the sea off local Ministry of Defence ranges] were about to return ashore in a small inflatable motor dinghy.

In the conditions prevailing Coxswain Richards decided to escort them to safety, so the Lifeboat put to sea straight away.

As the inflatable boat ran in towards the harbour and got within 200 yards of safety, a huge wave capsized the boat. The Lifeboat was at the scene within a couple of minutes and three men were pulled from the water. One man was trapped beneath the capsized boat and another was being dragged down by the boat's flexible fuel pipe, which had become entangled around his neck.

As Coxswain Joshua Richards skilfully held the Lifeboat in position with the heavy seas sweeping over her, Second Coxswain Alan Thomas leaned over the side and tried to feel for the trapped man. Eventually he felt the man's hand, grabbed it and dragged him onto the Lifeboat.

Emergency Mechanic Roy Young cut the fuel pipe which was trapping the fifth man, who was then pulled to safety.

An amazing rescue, saving five lives.

The problems with the Lifeboat House were quite serious and it was decided to place a new galvanised steel substructure beneath the Boathouse and also replace the Slip.

The new work was complicated by the fact that it had to be done without disturbing the Boathouse itself. The old wooden structure was subsequently removed.

The work was completed in spring 1980 at a cost of nearly £400,000. At the time it was the biggest single item of expenditure in RNLI history. An example of the costs the RNLI have to bear, completely from voluntary contributions.

In November 1982 **William Alan Thomas** (son of former Coxswain William Ray Thomas) was appointed Coxswain of the Tenby Lifeboat.

He succeeded Coxswain Josh Richards (son of former Coxswain Thomas Benjamin Richards).

Prior to the establishment of Tenby's first Lifeboat Station in 1852, Alan Thomas' great-great-grandfather John Ray was awarded the Honorary Medallion of the Royal Humane Society following the sloop *Mary* being wrecked off Tenby in November 1834.

54 A TENBY LIFEBOAT FAMILY

So is the family lineage passed down through the generations in Tenby. They serve with pride, devotion to duty and honour.

Working in union with the Inshore Lifeboat, whenever occasion demands, Coxswain Alan Thomas, Motor Mechanic Charles Crockford and their crew have attended many rescues.

Henry Comber Brown was launched in the early morning of Sunday 25th September 1983 after it was reported that the yacht *Sailing Bye* had dragged her anchor and run aground on the North Beach.

As Alan Thomas was absent, Second Coxswain John John was in command of the Lifeboat as they headed to the casualty.

In choppy seas and a force five onshore wind, the 27ft yacht was aground 400 yards from the Lifeboat Station, lying broadside on to a heavy surf, she was listing heavily to starboard and being pounded by the waves. There were two men and three children on board.

By skilful use of his engines, Acting Coxswain John John held the Lifeboat in position and a small inflatable dinghy, carried on the Lifeboat, was veered down towards the yacht, being manned by crew members Nicky Crockford (son of Lifeboatman Flanagan Crockford) and Nicholas Tebbutt.

They reached the yacht safely by 5:07 am and made a towline fast aboard the yacht.

Acting Coxswain John John took the Lifeboat slowly ahead, to hold the yacht steady while the inflatable was worked around the stern and the youngest of the children, aged nine, was taken off. The two Lifeboatmen were closer to the beach than they were to the Lifeboat and so they rowed ashore and handed the child into the care of the Coastguard.

The two crewmen then prepared to relaunch the inflatable dinghy, and with Nicholas Tebbutt at the oars, Nicky Crockford remained in the water to steady the boat. Just as they were setting off through the heavy surf a very large wave struck the inflatable and capsized it. The two crewmen quickly righted it, but decided to push the boat out through the surf to the casualty.

With one man either side of the boat this was successfully done, both men being frequently totally submerged. The other two children were ferried safely ashore and handed over to the Coastguard at 5:20 am.

Throughout the rescue, Acting Coxswain John John had held the *Henry Comber Brown* in position, steadying the yacht with the tow-line and illuminating the scene of rescue with the Lifeboat's searchlight.

Once the children were safe he began to tow the yacht into deeper water, the two men remaining on the yacht throughout this operation.

The yacht was secured to a mooring outside Tenby harbour at 5:30 am and the Lifeboat placed on her moorings as it was too rough to rehouse her.

For this service the RNLI's Thanks on Vellum was awarded to Nicky Crockford and Nicholas Tebbutt.

A framed letter of thanks, signed by the Chairman of the RNLI, His Grace the Duke of Atholl, was sent to the Acting Coxswain John John.

On Lifeboat Day, August 2nd 1986, the Inshore Lifeboat, crewed by helmsman Denny Young and crewmen John John, Bobby James and Roy Young rescued a man from rocks at Monkstone Point in rough sea and gale force winds. All four were awarded the RNLI's Thanks on Vellum.

The current Motor Mechanic of Tenby Lifeboat, **Charles Crockford**, took over in 1973. Nephew of Ivor Crockford and a seaman born and bred. To date [1999] he must be Tenby's longest serving Motor Mechanic, having already served some twenty-six years. He has served with Coxswain Josh Richards and Coxswain Alan Thomas. He has attended many rescues, a notable one in 1982 in the 'relief' Inshore Lifeboat.

Two boys were cut off by the tide at Freshwater East. Notorious for its currents, which have been known to take a child off the beach, it is some eight miles west of Tenby.

The boys were sheltering in a gully at the foot of the cliffs in a force four south-west breeze and heavy six foot swell.

Finding it impossible to take the ILB directly to them, Coxswain Alan Thomas ran her up to the rocks and Charles Crockford leapt for shore. By jumping from rock to rock he reached the two boys, helping them one at a time back on board the ILB.

An exceptionally high wave threatened to sweep the ILB, containing the Lifeboatmen and the boys, against the rocks. Coxswain Alan Thomas just succeeded in clearing them fully before the wave swept in.

The boys were put ashore at Freshwater East after a rescue that lasted two hours. The ILB then returned to Tenby Harbour. The RNLI's Thanks on Vellum was awarded to Coxswain Alan Thomas and Motor Mechanic Charles Crockford for this service.

On September 29th 1986 a new Tenby Lifeboat was commissioned and named in a ceremony at Tenby Harbour by HRH Princess Alexandra, with the band of the Welsh Guards and a detachment of Gurkhas, the ***RFA Sir Galahad***.

A steel hulled 47 foot Tyne class, self-righting Lifeboat built at a cost of £494,000 provided out of funds raised by members of the Royal Fleet Auxiliary, by a number of gifts and legacies, and by a local appeal launched by the then Honorary Secretary Mr Eric Bancroft.

She was named after the Royal Fleet Auxiliary *Sir Galahad* which was severely damaged and suffered heavy casualties in the Falkland's War in 1982. It was hoped that the Tenby Lifeboat ***RFA Sir Galahad*** would serve as a fitting memorial to the gallantry of the dead and wounded of her namesake, and members of the Falkland's Families Association attended the ceremony.

TENBY LIFEBOAT ROLL OF HONOUR

1835
Honorary Medallion of the Royal Humane Society
to John Ray

1856
Silver Medals to Lieutenant Jesse (Chief of Coastguards) and to
Coxswain Robert Parrott

1859
Silver Medals to Lieutenant Boyle (Chief of Coastguards) and
Coxswain Robert Parrott

1875
Silver Medal to Coxswain Thomas Monger
for Long Service

1938
Silver Medal to Acting Coxswain John Rees and Bronze Medal to
Motor Mechanic Alfred Cottam

1953
Silver Medal to Thomas Richards and Bronze Medals to Bowman
William Thomas and Motor Mechanic William Rogers

1966
Silver Medal and Maud Smith Award to Crewman Michael
Wilson, and Bronze Medal to Bowman Josh Richards

1981
Bronze Medal to Coxswain Josh Richards

1989
Silver Medal and Maud Smith Award to Coxswain Alan Thomas

*(**Publisher's note:** The history of the Tenby Lifeboat (1986 - present) continues in the **Epilogue**. Further information about Tenby RNLI can be found on the Internet at*
www.tenby-lifeboat.co.uk *- and at **www.rnli.org.uk** is the RNLI headquarters' homepage).*

ONE OF THE MOST BEAUTIFUL

No one could ask to be born in a more beautiful town than Tenby, one of the most beautiful resorts in the British Isles. It has great antiquity.

It came into prominence eight hundred years ago, after the Norman occupation of South Pembrokeshire.

William de Valence and his wife Joan, Earl and Countess of Pembroke, granted Tenby a Charter around 1290. It was part of their estate.

When given over to the people, a common council was formed. It became a borough and burgesses of land were distributed.

Bailiffs were appointed to oversee law and order. The burgesses were a privilege given to a townsman in return for some duty he had performed satisfactorily for the Lord.

The arable land surrounding the town ran from areas such as 'The Norton' and 'The Green.' The River Ritec, along the Marsh Road, would have been a tidal estuary at this time.

Each burgess was a strip of land, long and narrow, as land was scarce on such a rocky promontory. It was named after the person to whom it was granted. The names are still there to some extent, and Alan and myself were born on one such burgess strip. 'Broadwell,' 'Maudlins,' 'Heywood' all now used as road names; and many more too to retain our history.

When the Earl and Countess of Pembroke were deceased, their heirs confirmed that these land privileges could continue, and indeed enlarged upon them.

Pasture to graze animals close to the fortressed town was scarce. Fresh meat, milk and vegetables, wheat, corn and barley, all were necessary to provide for the inhabitants.

ONE OF THE MOST BEAUTIFUL 59

What a hive of industrious people it must have been. Many workshops would have been necessary. Blacksmiths, farriers, stables, farms, agriculture, all leading up to the little town.

Some of the gentry of the day lived on the outskirts. Scotsborough House on the road to Gumfreston, and Trefloyne near Penally are examples.

Tenby's privileges were confirmed by several Kings of England and in 1402 King Henry IV gave them the right to choose a Mayor. This privilege has been exercised ever since. Nearly six hundred years. It is to the credit of Tenby Town Council that a record of our Mayors has been kept since the year of that first appointment.

In the Middle Ages, Tenby was a busy port trading with France, Spain and Portugal. High tide saw a hive of activity as laden sailing ships entered and left the harbour.

Her townsmen were seamen venturing out to the wider world. Her townsmen were fishermen fighting the elements to secure food.

Hardworking, but happy within their united environment, the townsmen were to suffer from pillaging and looting in 1260 when it was sacked in the uprising led by Llywelyn ap Gruffydd, siege by Oliver Cromwell during the Civil War [he had his headquarters at Trefloyne] and Plague.

Tenby later rose to fame as a fashionable watering place. Edwardian and Georgian houses were built, accompanying the old merchants' houses and fishermen's cottages.

Our finest antiquity is our Parish Church, Saint Mary's, dated from the thirteen century, but probably even earlier. It has been enlarged from time to time to accommodate its population. Very spacious, very beautiful, influenced by the continued history of its townsmen. Wealthy or poor it has always been there as a haven and, in keeping with Tenby's nautical tradition, to seamen its spire is a landmark.

My brother Alan and I are very proud to have been christened there in the 1930s. My sister Peggy married there at the end of the War, and some years later my dear friend Wendy Nowell was to marry there and have her children christened. Her husband John has done some beautiful woodwork in the Church.

Whatever one's beliefs, our Churches provide a sense of purpose in life, unity, belonging and pride. I feel Saint Mary's is one of the most beautiful Churches and a great credit to Tenby and its people who so generously support it.

Some important dignitaries of the town lived at the top of our road and as they seldom used cars we saw them walk past daily; so we became familiar with them.

Mrs Margaret Jane Jenkins, known as Jane, lived in a detached house which was directly in line with our road, but actually situated on the Serpentine. She also owned land there and was very generous in allowing others to use it.

Born in 1873, she married in 1898 at the age of twenty-five. She had one son and three daughters. She and her husband formed a company, J Jenkins and Co.

Jane Jenkins became a Councillor in 1921 and was elected Mayor in 1927. In 1932 she became an Alderman of Tenby and Justice of the Peace. One of her married daughters, Anne Norman, also became a Councillor.

In her field, facing her house, there was a stile and footpath leading to the woods, which we used at every opportunity, as Box Wood and Folly Wood were our treasured playground.

She also had a field in line with her house which she allowed to be used annually by the Boy Scouts for their camp and jamboree. On one occasion we were lucky enough to be invited. A large bonfire was lit in the centre of the camp. The scoutmasters and scouts, all in uniform, sat in a tidy circle around it with crossed legs. We were placed in-between as guests. One scout took the lead in singing and we learned, as we went along, all the traditional scout songs. It was such united fun. Midsummer's Night, turning dark before we left, the smoke from the fire, and all faces

ONE OF THE MOST BEAUTIFUL

reflected in its flickering light, made it a memorable occasion.

I suppose I was about seven or eight and I quite liked the handsome Boy Scout sitting next to me. He has held my hand when we were singing. I went home strangely moved. Only to be devastated the next day when I saw him talking to a little fair-haired girl from Newell Hill. Oh, the pains of youth!

Also, at the top of our road was the large detached house "Belvedere." This was the gracious home of a gracious family, Mr and Mrs T P Hughes.

Thomas Phillip Hughes was born in 1867, son of Mr and Mrs John Hughes.

Mr Thomas Hughes, draper and house furnisher in Tenby, highly respected townsman, for many years their name has been synonymous with Tenby High Street and Upper Frog Street. In 1900 at the age of thirty-three years, he married Nancy Watt. They had two sons, Tom and David, and a daughter, Mary.

Mr Thomas Hughes became a Councillor in 1919 at the age of forty-two. He polled the highest number of votes ever recorded in the Borough. He was particularly interested in matters of progress in the town: housing for its poor and advertising it as a tourist destination. He was elected as Mayor in 1925 when he was fifty-eight years old and he was made an Alderman of the town in 1926.

Outside the grounds of their house was a public leisure area with seats. This was one of our favourite meeting and play places as we could use the seats in our games as beds, or as stages for our singing and dancing.

Young Tom Hughes and his sister, Mary, often came to the hedge to watch us and talk to us. They gave us apples from the orchard and played conkers with us. They weren't allowed out to play as we were. David, the youngest, was just a toddler. My sister Peggy was later to become his

HE CALLED ME HIS MONA LISA

1939 was an eventful year for me. I started school although still a few weeks off my fourth birthday. It was September and the start to the new school year.

A hectic Monday morning getting the children into action after the long summer holiday; I started to cry, my mother asked: "Why?"

I said: "Everyone is going to school except me."

My mother said: "Look my girl, if you can find yourself a pair of shoes in that cupboard, you can go."

The shoe cupboard on the side of the fireplace was an unbelievable jumble. It had a strong leather smell. The assortment of shoes to fit the family were very shabby. Size One - I was limited in choice, but I did find a little pair of red ones that went on my feet.

My sister Joyce was told to take me by the hand all the way to headmaster Ossie Morgan's study and ask if it was permissible for me start as I was really too young.

I can remember every detail of my first day, and how wonderful it seemed to me. Joyce explained that I very much wanted to come to school. Ossie eyed me, lifted me up in his arms and took me to a glass fronted cupboard, where he selected a coloured pencil and envelope, going back to his desk, he stood me down.

He scribbled on the envelope and said: "If you can do that you can start."

I suppose he wanted to see if I could hold a pencil; I said: "Please sir I can do better than that, I can write my name."

And Joyce said "Yes sir and she can tell the time, and read Jack the Ripper books."

I wish I could remember his facial expression at this retort. Joyce was into reading Jack the Ripper stories and as I often sat near her when she was reading and having been told to be quiet, I started reading as well. What assorted knowledge I imbibed I don't know, as I was slow and Joyce turned the page before I was finished.

I was taken to the Infants' Class. Which had sweet little desks with seats that lifted up and down. The pretty lady teacher was Miss Thomas. My father bought his daily newspaper from her father's shop in Tudor Square. She was quite tall with black hair arranged in pinned curls around her face. She wore a beautiful blue dress. Her classroom cupboard was so nice, she had painted it with symbols of the alphabet. A is for apple, B is for ball ... and learning and writing on a slate with chalk was great, if you did make a mistake you just licked your finger and rubbed it out.

We had one boy in the class, who I was afraid of. I won't name him although we knew him well. He obviously had a learning problem which resulted in forceful anger from time to time: whoever was nearest bore the brunt, teacher or pupil. His ignorance of ability to handle anything out of the norm seems incredible to us today. But we must remember that there were no special schools for children with special needs. But Miss Thomas was patient. When he wished to go to the toilet she undid his trouser buttons and braces, and off he went running across the playground (to the children's outside toilets) hanging onto his falling pants, braces dangling. Her method of control, when he was unruly, was to struggle with him and place him within the heavy metal fireguard where he had to stay in disgrace. She never smacked him to my knowledge. As he was not forward enough to move up in class she had to endure this for some years.

For school my long hair, which I could sit on, was plaited in two thick plaits each of which was tied with any old bit of rag handy. Bits were torn off old dresses and kept for this purpose. Our income did not aspire to hair ribbons. This particular boy loved to catch me by the plaits and swing on them like ropes.

I had encountered this behaviour before starting school, if my mother sent me to Fanny Davies' shop on the Green for bread. I had to take a stick to fend him off. Or sometimes our dog, which in my little mind was hopefully going to gobble him up. But I did acquire a device against the demon. It was a wart that grew on one of my fingers. My sisters scorned it when washing me as it was said if you touched it you also got one. What we believed in our ignorance was nobody's business. This came to my aid in confrontation. I faced him and said that I would touch the end of his nose with it, and he would have a big one grow, right on the tip. It worked a treat.

One little girlfriend I had, a policeman's daughter who lived up the Jubilee [a cul-de-sac with its entrance just down our road] had a Grandma who could charm warts. It seems she had already cleared the stricken milkman's hands completely. Playing in her house one day her Granny asked that I should be brought to her sitting room. She asked if I would like her to charm my wart away, but I was frightened and put my hand behind my back. She smiled and said that if I would just show it to her she wouldn't say anything. So I gave her my little hand and she just patted it, and off home I went. Do you believe in Fairy Stories? I do because later when I was looking for some doll's clothes in the bedroom drawer I discovered I'd lost my wart. I was panic stricken for a moment, doll's clothes forgotten. I was looking for my wart, there was a big hole in my knuckle, where it had been, and I thought I'd die! Associated with witchcraft there was a lot of old wives' tales, which we children believed anyway. But I was rid of my ugly wart.

About this time a dear eccentric old gentleman came into our lives. At the end of the Maudlins' council houses there is a row of semi-detached private houses, the first one of these was owned to begin with by the Lillicrops, the town's

HE CALLED ME HIS MONA LISA

fishmongers. I was friends with the little girls, Jocelyn and Margaret, and was sad when they moved away. Into this same house came Dr Hogan. He was a child's ideal as a grandad, soft white hair around a balding round head, a clean pink face with twinkling eyes, one of which held a monocle which hung around his neck on a leather thong. He always wore a black beret straight across his forehead, which he only took off when sitting to our table. He carried a knobbly walking stick, his trousers and jacket were thick and baggy, his clean shirt worn without a collar.

An arrangement was made between himself and my mother that she should act as his housekeeper for which he would pay her a small wage. Money was always needed, and to give her credit she took this task on her shoulders in a conscientious way. For her convenience he ate at our house, alone, and lived in his house. He loved children and wanted us in the room with him, so we used to sit quietly on the mat whilst he slurped his oatmeal and read his paper through his monocle, propped up on the HP sauce bottle. Oatmeal was never made for anyone else but him. Neither were artichokes etc which he loved, and mother cooked for him.

He had been a doctor out in Africa and had come to Tenby to retire. Like us he walked the woods and shores. In his house, which mum had to keep clean, the furnishings were sparse but good. A huge table stood alone in the sitting-room and it was covered with books. He slept in the back bedroom. As he became enfeebled later, mum saw him to bed and up in the morning. The front bedroom contained a suite and the bed made up in case he was ill. Mum and one of us for company would sleep there to keep watch, as on one occasion he had got up in the night and fallen down stairs; there was no stair-carpet and he was badly bruised.

This dear old man, who had some bossy sisters, was eventually put in a nursing home. My mother fought against it, but to no avail. We were all heartbroken, he died the same year. He left us some money in his will. One hundred pounds for mother and fifty pounds for each child. To give mother her due, she spent it on clothes for each of us. Oh to own two dresses, a coat and mac and strong shoes was unbelievable. Unfortunately the shoes hurt, as by then my feet had got used to stretchy 'scruffies.'

Even in such a large family, each child is a different individual from the next, eager to learn but resilient to forceful influence. Strictly brought up, well-mannered, we lived side by side without a lot of disharmony. Our sisters and brother our friend and so it has remained. All of us wanting to be independent above all, but turning to and receiving love and help from each other at different times, through our lives. No matter how many years go by, to meet is to be back on our old level.

How sad that we never had the opportunity to re-embrace our father in this way. I suppose in a way Tenby has become our shrine for him, and to go back to visit is to go back to our childhood. Walks along the North Beach to see dad at the Lifeboat Station ... and ask his permission for whatever, we would never have dreamed of operating without it. Money was short so we knew not to ask for it. But so many of our pleasures cost nothing, so that was no hardship, and the War years were lean for everyone, most of our friends didn't have a lot more than us. Those who were well off, didn't seem snobbish, we were invited into their homes and given a share at tea-time.

As we all progressed through school (one or two years ahead of the next) between us we were, amongst all the other children in the town of school age, known as one of the Cottams.

During the War teachers were scarce but Wales is a nation of schoolteachers and we were well blessed. Ossie Morgan our headmaster held in high regard, strict but fair with a genuine love of children, he played host to evacuees in his own home. He had a fine singing voice, and always took us himself for music.

HE CALLED ME HIS MONA LISA 67

Ensor Morgan was a fine man. Home from the War he took over Standard Three when I was there, the first day in class I remember this handsome man with thick dark curly hair and a decidedly auburn moustache: a fly kept landing on it first one side then the next, so gently and so many times he brushed it off. As he discovered my leaning to Literature and Art we became friends, he didn't have any children of his own. He called me his Mona Lisa, because of my features and my long thick hair, he used to ask me to sit and read to him while he marked our books.

It took quite a time in the mornings, getting the gang together for our short walk to school. As we lived at the top of the road, the onus was on us to do the calling as we went down.

We always went to the back door of the house, which invariably led straight into the kitchen to call for our friends. The Lillicrops, who lived opposite, had two little girls, Jocelyn and Margaret. They were sweet children. Better off than us. But they loved to be included in our group. Their mother was a very pretty lady and made us most welcome. She used to take me to the beach with them and even made me a little swimsuit to keep for the occasion. If the girls weren't ready when I called I was allowed to play with their dolls in the conservatory until they had finished their breakfast. They had so many lovely things and I would be lost for a little while, putting the dolls in and out of prams and remaking it.

Margaret, the youngest one, was fairly delicate and to protect her from the cold, her mother put leather gaiters on her little legs before she left for school. These were brown polished leather that fitted from ankle to knee, fastened with little tiny buttons and loops. Her mother used a button hook, something we don't see today and probably just as well. Margaret hated wearing them and cried a bit whilst she sat on the bottom of the stairs for this procedure. I didn't even have socks and wore worn out sandals on my little feet. But oh boy, did I feel lucky!

Each house we went to call for a friend was slightly different, and they would be at various stages of preparation for school. Sometimes we waited on the step and sometimes we were asked in while Mrs Nowell put the ribbon in Wendy's hair or Margaret Pullin finished her breakfast. I didn't like the thought of being there if they were eating bread and milk, 'pobs' as it was called, it was white and sloppy and had a yeasty smell. It was often given to children as a breakfast dish with a little sugar sprinkled on top. Always we had to be fed on what was available and certainly during the War there were few breakfast cereals that we knew of. Those who had 'pobs' loved it. I hated the thought of it, however hungry I was.

Other than this you had porridge. Equally horrid to me. Or a slice of bread and jam or dripping. The dripping, which was kept in the pantry in an earthenware jar, was collected fat from the home roasting and very precious it was. The flavour varied as you went down the jar depending on what the meat had been. Beef, lamb or pork. Another fat in daily domestic use was goose grease. As the only chance to collect this was Christmas when you might have a goose - they were more common in those days than turkey. The grease was collected during cooking. A goose gives off a lot of grease.

This was considered a health aid. It was not eaten but stored in old jam jars and kept, to be rubbed into the chest if you had a cold or chest complaint, backache or chilblains. We had plenty of chilblains, not having socks in winter. If we had a cough my mother would slice onions in a vegetable tureen, sprinkle it with sugar and then pour hot malt vinegar over it, the lid was put on and a dessert spoon put by the side. If we coughed in the night we just helped ourselves to a spoonful of the vinegar juice which was the only medicine we ever had and saw us through croup and colds. But because we were so hardy we didn't get much. Goose grease was always shared with the neighbours.

Once our merry band had gathered, off we tripped to school. I don't know what it was about the Maudlins, but most people walked down the middle of the road. Few motor cars to worry about then.

On we skipped, on and off the pavement, and walked along the top of any suitable wall, jumped over any post low enough and giggling and chattering up Greenhill Road. Sometimes this last bit had to be done at a run as we could hear the school bell being rung.

The playground would be full of children waiting, albeit reluctantly to go into school and their play would be halted by the teacher, taking line duty, ringing the large brass hand bell which had a polished wooden handle. The children then ran and formed lines, each within their own class. These were straightened and hushed before we filed into school, to the cloakroom and the assembly hall for Prayer. Late comers dashed down the school steps and anxiously joined their lines.

Prayers started the day. The Infants' Class was at the front and so the stages of classes ranged towards the back. The teacher of each class sat at the end of the row to keep order, and prefects (children selected from the top class, Standard Five) stood by the radiators to assist the teacher in spotting any naughty behaviour.

Our headmaster, Ossie Morgan, walked with some majesty to take Prayers ... "Good morning children." In chorus we returned: "Good morning Mr Morgan." He held us with his strict countenance, but I always felt he had a hidden smile within his soft mouth and a twinkle in his eye. He had the most wonderful voice, speaking and singing. He taught us himself in singing lessons and tried to teach us to project our voices up into the mouth and over the roof of it to create tone.

I feel musical ability, like art, is something you can improve on, if you already have some talent. But we were very fortunate in our wonderful teacher and loved singing. Our Prayer was the Lord's Prayer every day, which we spoke aloud together. Our hymns varied from time to time. The favourites were "All things bright and beautiful, all creatures great and small" and "There is a green hill far away, without a city wall." What were they talking about! It was here in Tenby. Our school was on the Greenhill.

Our teachers at this time were: Miss Thomas, Infants; Mrs Wright, Standard One; Miss Wright, Standard Two; Ensor Morgan, Standard Three; Miss James Standard Four; Mr Williams, Standard Five. One teacher per class.

The only times we were taken by others was singing with Ossie Morgan when two classes merged into one: much to our amusement, as this meant three to a desk instead of two. One had to sit on the gap in the middle, and being small it was usually me, where I got nudged for any wriggling from their bony elbows and still daren't make a sound or it might have been the cane.

Miss James took us for sewing. Once again, two classes in one. She was very much the epitome of a schoolteacher, and seldom seemed to have to discipline us. This might have been because it was a girls only class! The boys had woodwork and our hands were busy trying to tack and stitch a straight seam, or embroider chain stitch.

All work was inspected with an eagle eye, and you were told to unpick and restitch anything that did not come up to standard. Turning corners was very tricky.

The simple things we made were tray cloths, aprons, dolly bags, and by Standard Three we were even on to summer dresses. We all had a turn on the sewing machine, but mostly we hand-stitched in a double seam manner. No raw edges inside. We were given a choice of fabric for the dresses. The pretty pattern was tiny poppies, the same pattern, but three different colour mutations.

HE CALLED ME HIS MONA LISA 71

As you had to pay for the material I was only allowed one and opted for the red poppies with green leaves. I hoped I could do it justice. Some of the older girls helped us cut them out on Miss James' big flat desk top, whilst we stood by holding the pins.

So exciting it was when we were ready to start the shoulder seams of the bodice, first inserting the puffed sleeves, the most tricky part, and then gathering the skirt and tacking it on. I'm sure mine had more than its share of gathers here and there, and nearly came down to my ankles when I first tried it on, but standing on a chair this was adjusted by another girl pinning up the hem to the right length. We then had to make a sash, which caused some amusement as we ended up with a long tube inside out and had to devise a method of turning it the right way through the small opening at one end. Once again I gained from my sisters at home and used a ruler to push it through which did the trick. New school dresses in matching patterns we had made ourselves, at the age of nine. What an achievement.

Once or twice a year we had a little Concert or Play. Somehow I always seemed to be involved. On one occasion three of us were sent up into the loft to look for various costume items that we needed for the Play.

Used to going up the loft at home, but only when dad was out as it was his sanctuary, I walked along the beams as a tightrope to get from box to box. The boy who was with us thought this looked fun, fell off the beam and put his foot through the ceiling of Standard Five. We were in a state of hysteria as we dared to kneel down and peep through the hole. Mr Williams was seething beneath. Somewhat dusty.

How we got back down the ladder I don't know, but Miss James took the blame as she had sent us up. So we didn't get the cane.

In one Play I was dressed up as an old lady. Getting my thick plaits under the grey wig was a struggle and I ended up with my very small body draped in a woolly shawl. Tiny face and big grey head. I was rather proud of the fact that my doll was being used as the baby. She was also wrapped in a shawl. I called her Charmaine which was a name I had read in a book and seemed grand enough for her. I wouldn't have possessed her, except that my Joyce won her in a raffle.

I had practised my words very carefully. Loving poetry, this wasn't difficult. So I thought I'd intone my voice to that of an old lady. I stood in front of the mirror, one of my favourite places on a wet day, and pulled my face until I got a shaky voice.

As the Play was acted without a raised stage I had to come in through the classroom door from the corridor when given my cue. The blinds were drawn on the classroom windows and I had to hold a lighted candle in the candleholder with one hand and hobble on a walking stick with the other, doing both with shaky hands to add to the aged look. I started my dialogue but somehow spluttered with my speech and blew the candle out! Utter silence for a second whilst I froze in the complete darkness. Then roaring laughter and tongue in cheek applause until the class was hushed and my candle re-lit. Not sure then if it was a comedy or a drama, but I was quite popular in the playground at playtime.

THE WAR

Now comes the most vital event for on September 1st 1939 Germany invaded Poland and War was to be declared.

Every person living was to be affected to some degree. We living in Tenby were so fortunate compared with many. On September 3rd Great Britain and France declared War on Germany for this action. In the previous month Russia had entered into an alliance with Germany and so Poland came to be divided between them.

In all homes we had to be silent during news' broadcasts, now all on the radio was of great importance. Dad was extra busy with his radio repairs as no one wanted to miss anything, and households seldom had more than one set.

Our little town rose to the occasion as she always has. Although used to catering for holiday-makers, she now had to apply her hospitality in many directions. She was in a position to act as a solace and haven to the many troops and homeless people who were to flock into her small streets.

Our shoreline to some extent made us vulnerable. So the South Beach and Burrows' sand dunes [only planted with bracken after the War] were laid with mines and barbed wire. As many locals will know this was not a deterrent to us children, as we played games tiptoeing over them, excited by the danger. It is only now as adults, we grit our teeth at the thought.

Being near Pembroke Dock we had to be aware that we might be bombed or gassed. We were issued with gas masks. Dad wrote in copperplate writing each child's name and address on the brown cardboard boxes they came in, these had little straps which we hung around our necks. As my brother Alan and I were under five, we were given special Mickey Mouse ones. These were designed so as not to frighten small children and were red and black with a Mickey Mouse face on them. I shall never forget the hot rubber smell as they were pulled over our faces, they expanded and contracted as you breathed, the air being filtered through a perforated disc at the bottom. A short experiment was enough, I was glad I never had to wear one long-term. Indeed as we became more self-assured they were put to one side.

The town's Civil Defence was instigated, a band of volunteers, townsmen and women not going into the Forces. Some of the men were formed as Air Raid Wardens. At night they inspected the houses all over town, to see that no chink of light was visible from any house window. If there was, your door was knocked and you were told to put it right. This was the black-out as it was called, and from a household point of view it was horrendous. Seaside houses' high windows all had to be clad with black curtains. None available in any shop even if you had the money. The ironmongers in Upper Frog Street [nowadays the arcade that runs through the Town Walls, the modern location of a public house with the name of the Prince of Wales] had difficulty keeping up with the demand for black dye. All household wash-boilers, usually used for snow white sheets, were now turned black whilst the sheets and other curtains were dyed black and hung at windows.

Most street lights were no longer used. A trip to Fecci's for fish and chips on a dark night, meant hopping along with one foot on the curb and one on the road to find our way. We must have looked odd, but children just take it all on board and laugh. One night I thought I had been captured, as I was suddenly held back. It turned out that my plait had been caught on an iron railing. Oh, what a fright!

We avidly watched the phases of the moon, as this was our only night-light, inside our bedroom or outside. Sometimes we were allowed to use our dad's torch, but batteries were scarce and this was only for emergency. The self-made lamp he used for his night calls to the Lifeboat Station was a wooden varnished box with a large lamp front, it had a brass hinged lid with brass hook fastener, where the rechargeable radio battery was housed; it was too heavy for us children to lift and we were forbidden to touch it because of its importance.

A survey of the town's vacant room space took place. Tenby was told to expect an allotted number of evacuees and troops to be billeted. First Aid Posts and Home Guard Units were set up and any adult with free time enrolled, and was trained to perform a useful civil service to deal with the relevant problems. The camaraderie was tremendous, and helped all to cope. It made a pleasure of a chore.

Some larger houses were requisitioned for Government use. Sion House between the Norton, Gas lane and the Croft [since 1961 the site of Croft Court multi-storey flats] was the mortuary, as it had deep basements. Unbeknown to us children, one day out playing with some of our boyfriends, we entered the almost derelict upper part to play on a swing rope, erected by someone over a large hole in the staircase. We took it in turns to swing quite happily, although we were a bit frightened in the large empty house. It wasn't until later, when one of the boys told his elder brother that we had found a new play place, that we were told that there were dead bodies in the basement, it was enough to stop our antics. However well brought up we were we still did wrong at times.

Women were enlisted into the Fire Service as Auxiliaries. Also, women were enrolled to look after expected evacuees, who would be parent-less, these would have to be found suitable homes and live as part of the resident's family. Houses suitable for this had to place cards in their windows.

Receiving areas were formed, and residents were urged to forfeit all excess bedding for this cause. This was to be handed in at the Post Office. We didn't have any spare room with our large family, indeed scarcely enough.

We were issued with Identity Cards and Ration Books. When these were enforced, they were a source of extra income for my mother. As children we were never given tea to drink. We drank water - the odd cup of cocoa, or half an Oxo cube, with a piece of bread as a filler. Mum then was able to sell our tea coupons to our richer neighbours, and the few shillings she received bought one of us a pair of shoes. I have never had a cup of tea in my life.

Any man between eighteen years and under fifty, was expected to enlist. It was a matter of pride when a man passed his medical 'A1' and was able to join the Services. Many of our school friends' brothers and fathers went to War.

Our father being with the Lifeboat was in a reserved occupation and so exempt. My two elder sisters, Dora and

Joyce, were expected to do War work. My sister Joyce joined the Wrens. She looked so smart in her navy uniform with a long white scarf. It broke my heart when she went away, as she shared her bed with me in the small bedroom. Privileged for the use of the older ones, but nearly always included a toddler. I kept her photo to kiss beneath my pillow. But I was soon joined by my next sister in line for the small bedroom, Peggy, who was equally kind to me.

My eldest sister Dora went to Birmingham to work on munitions. Training as an Industrial Engineer she worked for Cincinnati Milling Machines. She lodged with a family called Poole. They had a daughter Joan who was the same age. These young ladies became firm friends. Sharing the same work, home and leisure.

Joan came home with Dora on holiday twice a year. Which is my only recollection of Dora in my childhood as we were opposite ends of the family so to speak. I don't remember any personal contact with her. Her friendships with Joan Poole and her close friend at home, Gwyneth Bryn who lived across the road, have lasted a lifetime.

Everyone was encouraged to produce food in their gardens, some dug up the front lawn. Large posters saying 'Dig for Victory' were pasted on placards around the town.

In a subtle way, our lives were changing to quite a degree. By April 1940 the Germans had invaded Denmark and Norway. Six days later British Troops landed in Norway to keep the Germans back. One month later, May 10th, the Germans invaded Luxembourg, Holland and Belgium. Neville Chamberlain resigned and Winston Churchill became Prime Minister.

Within four days, on May 14th the Germans invaded France, the pace greater than any expectation. To make matters worse, the Italian dictator Mussolini declared War on the allies. By June 22nd France surrendered, becoming an occupied country just a few sea miles from our shores.

Ten days later, July 4th, German Blitzkrieg on Britain began with air battles over the English Channel as attacks were made on coastal convoys. Even the powers that be could hardly take it in. Five weeks later on the eve of *Aldertag* [13th August] Day of the Eagle operation by the German Luftwaffe, marked the start of the Battle of Britain proper. One thousand, four hundred and eighty-five German aircraft crossed the channel; to bomb our country.

But Hitler did not get it all his own way. After two months of British counter-attack Hitler cancelled his invasion plan for Britain and the Battle of Britain was won. No chance to be complacent as another five years of War were to ensue.

In 1940 we had Belgians, who had been evacuated from Dunkirk, together with some of our own British troops. These men together with other Belgian troops scattered about, were ordered to reform into a military unit. Their headquarters in Tenby was the Atlantic Hotel on the Esplanade. The Esplanade Hotel later became a secondary headquarters.

They were well received in the town. The men trained in the Tenby area, into the 1st Belgian Fusiliers, which then took its place in the British Order of Battle. They left Tenby in 1941 eventually becoming the Belgian Liberation Brigade, which fought its way home from Normandy. How much they must have appreciated their respite in Tenby.

As children of the town with so much freedom, like little mice we got everywhere.

Having American forces come to town was exciting to us as we only saw the advantages of everything.

They had a social club just past the Royal Gate House Hotel. It had a shop front window with lace curtains. The lights were often on in the daytime, unlike ours as we had to watch the pennies. We often stood at the window and peeped in at the comfortable interior lounge chairs and bar.

The first Christmas they were in Tenby they gave a party and a cross-section of the town were given invitations. One

American soldier called to our school and gave our headmaster Ossie Morgan four invitation tickets for the party.

How was he to allocate them without favouritism? Must have been a dilemma and he was a fair man. He came up with an ingenious idea. Our school toilets in the playground were two flat roofed concrete buildings, one for the boys and one for the girls, with several small children-sized toilets in each. So many little 'tiddlers' using them, they were in constant need of attention.

With this in mind he came around the classes and asked for volunteers to clean the toilets. Our Beryl put her hand up. She would do anything to get out of school-work. She was given a ticket to go to the party and didn't even have to clean the toilets. Was she delighted!

In preparation for this event, an extra effort was needed with her appearance. As here was the tomboy of the family with no regard for her already poor clothes. Blessed with the biggest mass of fair curls and blue eyes she was an adorable mixture and very popular. The biggest problem was shoes as she had a tendency to walk over on them, as my mother put it. They were soon shabby and she could not borrow anyone else's. Her dresses often came apart at the seams as she did her Tarzan act of swinging from one tree branch to another, or her bareback horse-riding stunt, which left me with my mouth open as I was fairly scared to pat the nice horse on the nose. Fearless in all her escapades, she was my complete opposite. But good sister that she was, she stood in my defence on many occasions and has never lost her protective love towards me.

First her hair had to be washed in rain-water from the water-butt kept for this purpose. It was poured from a big china jug, freezing cold over your head in the bath. As your hair would have been washed in Lifebuoy medicated soap, red and strong smelling, the soap suds poured into your eyes if you weren't careful so we held a piece of flannel up to them to try to prevent this, as it did sting and make your eyes water. Shampoo was unheard of, in our house anyway.

Whilst her hair was still wet and manageable it would be wound around the finger into dozens of small ringlets. Ready at last and tidy for five minutes, off she went to the party. She had never been to one like it before. Everything arranged for their pleasure. Food and sweets flown from America, unlike any we had even before rationing. When leaving, the children were given a bag of sweets and chewing gum to take home. Which we shared as always, one each.

The American troops had quite an effect on the town. Confident and well-groomed they dominated the local social scene, which was naturally resented by a great many people.

My sisters Dora, Joyce and Peggy were attractive girls under twenty. They loved dancing and went whenever they could to the De Valence Pavilion, independent by their own earnings they didn't have to ask mother for the money. To my knowledge she never expected them to put money into the home. They were keeping themselves from the day they left school and that was enough. As they were generous and aware of what it was like to have nothing they often treated us little ones in small ways.

Going dancing was really something for Tenby girls at that time. With so many troops stationed around the area they had limitless choice of partners.

Fantastic dance bands toured the country for many years, creating the music for the dances of the day, and indeed for many years to come. The waltz, quickstep, fox-trot, tango, rumba, samba and the jive of the day, the Jitterbug, where the girl was literally thrown into various positions. Athletic but great fun for the dancers and those watching. The Americans were very adept at this. And the girls didn't want to get too involved with one partner. The protocol of a dance hall was such that unless you went with a partner of the opposite sex you sat with your girlfriends until a gentleman came and asked you to dance. May I have this dance please? It was up to you if you wished to accept or not depending on what you felt about him. Was he nice looking? Tall enough? Drunk? The girls had to judge. Could he dance? As the man had to lead in some very complicated dance steps the female was only as good as her partner when she followed through the body movements. As dancing was such a social asset most took the trouble to learn and perfect.

When the dance finished the gentleman escorted the lady back to her seat and said "Thank you." He would have to approach and ask again if he wanted the next one. Sometimes before the dance the bandmaster would announce that this was an 'excuse me' dance! And you got up with the knowledge that you may have a change of partner as another man who wanted to dance with you butted in and said, "Excuse me." All exciting fun, unless he trod on your feet. It was customary for a partner to ask if he may walk you home, and if you were smitten you were pleased to accept and when taken to your front door you could expect a kiss good night, and perhaps an arrangement to meet again. This was a socially accepted code of behaviour and it was a great advantage in helping young people form relationships as it gave a guideline. One knew what to expect. Our girls having gone with their sisters and friends knew they were not dependent on an escort to get home, so if they wished could be independent.

Of course, if a young man sets his sights on one particular girl this is not always easy and Peggy had one American admirer, Mickey Matthews. Based in Pembroke he was what in those days was called a half-caste. One parent white, one coloured. His own skin was an enviable tan. Curly hair and eyes black. He was very handsome. Peggy fell under his spell for a little while. Joyce kept a watchful eye.

Mickey Matthews had been away for a while and seen action in which he was wounded in the shoulder. He was being treated in the Army sick-bay. Peggy was telling Joyce about his injuries and showed Joyce an engagement ring she was wearing on a cord around her neck as mum and dad didn't know about it and she was only sixteen. Joyce stepped in and told Peggy that she couldn't go ahead with this engagement. She was too young and unworldly and mixed marriages had a lot of serious side effects. What would she do if she went to America as his wife and was unhappy? No money to get back home and Peggy had gone through school without learning to read and write.

Joyce said she would telephone the camp and ask to speak to Mickey Matthews telling him the engagement was off and that Peggy would post the ring back to him.

This she did, but he was not prepared to accept, and as soon as it was nightfall he got out of the camp sick-bay, through a bathroom window, and headed for our house.

I can remember him on the living roof sofa having the dressing changed on his shoulder as it was bleeding and had a black hole where a bullet had gone in.

Joyce took over from mother as she was known to have the strength and ability to cope. Anyway she persuaded him to accept the situation and leave before he implicated us in his desertion as to leave camp without permission was a serious matter. As the clock struck nine we children went up to bed. Not a moment before we hoped and not a moment after our parents hoped.

We were still awake in the darkened room when there was a loud knocking on the front door, and army boots clanging in the tiled porch. The GI Military Police had called to look for Mickey Matthews.

My father who had answered the door, and genuinely in the dark about the matter, said he didn't know what they were talking about but they were at liberty to search the house if they so wished.

So up and downstairs they marched shining large torches everywhere, as the only room which would have the gas lights on was the living room. We were not allowed them upstairs, only in our parents' bedroom.

When they entered our bedroom we were very frightened. Chosen for their stature they were big men and the military uniform with big boots and gaiters gave an added strength.

I was on the outside of the big bed. We girls slept three to a bed and Alan slept on his own, unless I had gone into his bed to read him his comics and fallen asleep.

They opened the wardrobe door and shone the torch inside and behind it, under the beds and on our small faces, marched back downstairs and we watched from the window as they drove off in their jeep.

What the outcome was as far as Mickey Matthews was concerned I don't know. Or what reprimand my sister got from dad. It was considered an adult matter and in our family you didn't ask questions.

Having the Americans come to Tenby was another change for the families of the town, as well as extra trade for the shops, pubs and businesses.

The local young ladies of the day were impressed with their high standards of dress and sophistication. They seemed like film stars straight off the screen. I suppose there are good and bad in all races. Moral standards of the day were high and any young lady seen to flirt with too many soon got a bad name.

One bungalow in Broadwell Hayes, the last one before the Jubilee, had steep steps up to it, and it was the home of a very nice couple: Mr and Mrs Pension. They had one daughter, Gwen, who was a similar age to my eldest sister Dora. They also had a similar appearance being tall and slim with red hair. They both married Americans.

Gwen fell in love with an American Officer and she married him at the Baptist Church in Deer Park. I had seen the trousseau before the wedding, which he had sent to America for. Choice was very limited on luxury items and they were extravagant on our ration book's clothing coupons.

Everything that Gwen was to wear on her wedding day was gold coloured satin, even the underwear which had 'Babe' embroidered on the French knickers and slip. The wedding dress was beautifully designed and embroidered with gold embroidery and tiny covered buttons on the bodice and long fitted sleeves. Her veil was golden coloured lace which went so well with her lovely auburn hair. We watched her go into Church on Mr Pension's arm and come out with her handsome husband. She went to America to live at the end of the War. And some years later I was devastated to hear she had been killed in a motor car accident. What a terrible tragedy.

In Tenby, as well as every other town in the land, we had our own Home Guard ... 'Dads' Army' ... A unique citizen army.

This was made up of townsmen in the age group of fifteen to sixty-five, who for various reasons were unable to join up for the regular forces, or were exempt from them because of the nature of their work. Some were farm-workers, specialists whom it was vital to keep at home and some who had failed their medical through asthma, or flat feet, slight deafness or short sight.

Out of pride and a sense of duty everyone who was capable wanted to take part and be seen to be doing their best to help to win the War.

By 1940 these men were prepared to use the few weapons they had to fend off the most mechanised army the world had ever seen. We have to see the humour of it. But in reality it was far from funny.

Most of the training took place in the woods and fields, as this was the place where they were most likely to encounter the enemy. They were taught the art of self-defence and camouflage. This had to be achieved by using the branches of trees, grasses, leaves and hessian sacking. Everything then was packaged in hessian sacking, from potatoes to sugar, flour and oats. As it was already the right colour it was a very useful commodity and it cost nothing. Around the home it was used for doormats, sandbags, shoulder wraps against cold and rain. Bleached it was used for pillow cases and aprons.

For the Home Guard who did not have much in the way of uniform, the idea was to cover as much of the body as possible with hessian sacking and greenery. Thus blending with the environment when lying in wait for the enemy.

We encountered them in the woods on one occasion and were rather frightened. They had one sack over their heads with just a small hole cut out for the eyes and mouth. Another big mail-bag over their bodies with neck and arm holes. This was trimmed overall with greenery and as some didn't own hob-nail boots they wore their 'wellies' with their trousers tucked in. Some appeared to hold guns. Others held garden tools in the gun position for practise.

We hid behind a tree for a while and then scampered off, before we were shot.

Even if there was not a direct invasion, the Home Guard was likely to encounter confrontation firsthand with the enemy in the form of German parachutists who may land in our fields. With the bombing raids on Pembroke Dock this was thought highly likely.

They had to train to face and capture a professional pilot of the German Air Force with the meagre equipment. What a task and how brave.

Church halls or pubs were generally used as the meeting place. In Tenby it was in the Conservative Club premises [now part of the Royal Lion Hotel] and in Pembrokeshire there were three battalions of Local Defence Volunteers, for which the War Office approved the title of Pembrokeshire Yeomanry. Of the five companies formed from the battalions, D company was recruited in Tenby and had its headquarters and indoor training hall at the Delphi Garage on the South Parade [a few buildings up from the War Memorial - now a video shop].

Their prime role was to delay the invader, denying him advance. This released the Army of static guard duty to

THE WAR 85

some extent. Enabling them to concentrate more fully on other vital matters.

In the first instance, the men themselves would have selected their Platoon Leader and Officers. If their hall didn't have a telephone, and many didn't, an arrangement had to be made with the nearest house owning one to take calls on their behalf and allow them usage over the twenty-four hour day.

Like Lifeboatmen, these honourable townsmen had to be there at all times. They were unpaid volunteers. With no ranks and virtually no public funds.

Basic items like typewriters, stationery, blankets, even toilet rolls had to be scrounged. How many wives of these noble men sat in the evenings making khaki finger-less mittens, socks and pullovers, hats and scarves. The children knitted or unpicked other garments so that they could be reused. Nothing was wasted. Paper bags and newspapers were cut into squares, a hole was made in one corner with a meat skewer and a piece of string was threaded through. This paper pad was hung by the toilet for use when toilet paper was not available. Newspaper was also folded into paper spills and kept in a pot on the hearth to be used instead of spending matches once the fire or gas was lit.

How inventive is the human mind when necessity demands it. A satisfaction was achieved by these simple tasks as one felt every little thing helped to win the War. Which of course it did. We were in it together. Doing our bit.

As Home Guards, apart from any dangerous encounters, these men who had already perhaps done a day's work before reporting for duty, office workers in exempt positions, grocers, butchers, telephonists, plumbers, or older military men, had to put in a lot of hard labour in order to achieve their object. Without any mechanical help or vehicles at their disposal, they often had to borrow the farmer's horse and cart to transport heavy things.

In the event of a plane coming down in our fields, anyone who knew about it went to the wreckage, regardless of danger. Here was bounty. Perhaps parachute silk to make curtains or underwear. Perspex from the broken windscreen and windows had a lot of practical applications. The only tool used to make things from it was a hot poker. As this material was our forerunner to plastic which was yet to come.

Behind each gallant man there is a woman backing him in what he does. Sometimes doing several jobs at once and, when finished, feeling they have achieved nothing.

Tenby wives decided to show a positive face and formed an unofficial 'Tenby Housewives Corps' to provide emergency supplies for people having to take to the Air Raid Shelters at a moment's notice when the siren went. You dropped what you were doing and went. Nearly fifty supply points were established around the town. No mean achievement, and when you think of the number of years that these things had to be maintained. Everyone worked very hard.

As time went on it became apparent to the hierarchy that the Home Guard were attempting the impossible, and they were affiliated into Country Regiments. By the end of 1941 it was no longer a voluntary service. Conscription had begun.

This had a double-sided effect as Army discipline and red tape deluged the platoon, and the attitude to their role changed and was less fulfilling. Although they now had weapons and orthodox uniform they felt they had lost their stand in their society to some extent. It was no longer a personal matter.

The Home Guard were no small band, they amounted to a million men across the country, and gave a great deal of necessary support and feeling of security to its own townsmen. They felt they had their own little army to defend them and slept better in their beds at night.

It was also a good training ground for young men under eighteen as they could join in preparation for conscription in the Army.

They acted as a back up for the Civil Defence Services. From all this hard work, on a social level they achieved a companionship amongst themselves. Some would be lonely as other family members had gone to War. They had football matches and whist drives to keep cheerful.

I cannot write about the War in Tenby without mentioning our neighbouring port of Pembroke Dock.

TENBY ROLL OF HONOUR

(Published with permission by the author from the Rector of Tenby Canon David Jenkins, with assistance from Wilf Hardy President of Tenby Royal British Legion)

WORLD WAR II

Royal Navy

Lieutenant Jack Cosby Mason
Lieutenant John S Adams
Sub-Lieutenant W L Horner
Chief Petty Officer J D Richards
Petty Officer W H Stubbs
Petty Officer Charles Page
Gunner Jeffrey Badham
Gunner Norman Haskell Thomas
Stoker Bernard Badham
Able-bodied Seaman Samuel S Lewis
Second Wireless Officer Richard James
Steward Lionel Clarke
Steward Eric H Clarke
Ordinary Seaman Colin Aveston Rees

Royal Marines
Lieutenant Jack G Jones
Marine Richard Charles A Nicholl

Royal Regiment of Artillery
Major Paul Parbury MC
Lieutenant J Michael Edwards
Battery Sergeant Major Charles Oliver Webb
Sergeant John Goodridge
Lance Bombardier William R Creese

Welch Regiment
Major Norman Evans

East Surrey Regiment
Major J W D Armstrong

Royal Engineers
Major R H Glue
Sapper Hanver Walters

Commandos
Lieutenant Frank Stanley Mason
Sergeant Major Frank Goodenough

Shropshire Regiment
Lieutenant E King

Lancashire Fusiliers Regiment
Company Sergeant Major Samuel O A Palmer

Welsh Guards
Guardsman Desmond C J John
Guardsman Frank Thomas

Federated Malay States Volunteer Force
Captain Kenneth Bancroft

26th Punjabi Regiment
Major John William Nicholas

2/13th Frontier Force Rifles
Captain H A S Cotterill

Somerset Light Infantry Regiment
Private Richard H Evans
Private Donald D C Lewis

East Kent Regiment 'The Buffs'
Private R Toms

Royal Armoured Corps
Private Archie Thomas

Royal Army Service Corps
Captain Roger Alexander Karran

Royal Electrical and Mechanical Engineers
Sergeant Kenneth Diment

Royal Tank Regiment
Sergeant E G Vare

Royal Air Force
Squadron Leader Lionel R Cohen
Flying Officer David G Evans
Pilot Officer Gerald Shaw
Pilot Officer Donald Grant
Pilot Officer John T Eshelby
Flight Sergeant Pilot Peter Oliver
Flight Sergeant David Robert Booker
Flight Sergeant William F C Claque
Sergeant Air Gunner George Griffiths
Sergeant Air Gunner Neville Warlow
Aircraftman 1 John Rees
Aircraftman 2 David Ernest Stewart Richards

Women's Auxiliary Air Force
Corporal Rowena Hulton

Air Raid Casualties
Mrs Annie Diana Thomas
Mr Ivor Brace
Police Constable George Davies
Sergeant Major Raymond Bloch
Miss Evelyn A King

Died in Concentration Camp
Mrs Louise Sinnett
Master Tony Sinnett

WORLD WAR I

Royal Navy
Lieutenant Commander D R Mason
Lieutenant W Borrowes
Fleet Sub-Lieutenant E J K Buckley
Warrant Officer A Rutherford
Petty Officer W J Richards
Petty Officer John P Richards
Petty Officer John A Morris
Petty Officer W H Lewis
Petty Officer T J Collacott
Chief Stoker J A Jones
Leading Seaman J Norrish
Able-bodied Seaman Charles W Howells
Able-bodied Seaman Alfred Leonard
Able-bodied Seaman G H Mathews
Able-bodied Seaman James Seaton
Able-bodied Seaman William Wickland
Stoker W Davies
Cook's Mate William Hodgson
Diver William Buley

10th Royal Hussars
Private William H Bodill

Northants Yeomanary
Private Arthur Smith

Pembroke Yeomanry
Corporal W A Smith

Royal Field Artillery
Lieutenant-Colonel John Plunkett Vernon Hawksley DSO
Driver Norman Green

Royal Garrison Artillery
Sergeant C Glencross
Gunner Lionel W R Benson
Gunner John Evans
Gunner H J Fouracre
Gunner W H Hurley
Gunner John Lloyd
Gunner Richard Nock
Gunner H A Rees

Honourable Artillery Company
Lance Corporal A H O Lea

Royal Engineers
Lieutenant Colonel H M Henderson
Second Lieutenant Foss H Brown
Corporal H Tudor Thomas
Sapper John A Davies
Sapper E Morley

Welsh Guards
Private C Jeffreys

King's Own (Royal Lancaster Regiment)
Private H T Nicholls

Royal Warwickshire Regiment
Private Arthur M John

Royal Fusiliers
Rifleman Walter Scott
Rifleman E G Stratford

King's (Liverpool Regiment)
Lance Corporal W G Evans

Lincolnshire Regiment
Second Lieutenant R J Huntington

Somerset Light Infantry
Captain D Kenworthy
Second Lieutenant A Owen

Leicestershire Regiment
Lance Corporal H P Thomas

Cheshire Regiment
Private Wilfred Thomas

Royal Welch Fusiliers
Second Lieutenant A G Lord
Sergeant G T Wickland
Lance Corporal William E Glinn
Lance Corporal D Ackland
Private E J Cutcliffe
Private William John
Private H Kingston

South Wales Borderers
Captain J A Jones
Captain D C Parry Davies
Company Sergeant Major W H McGrath
Private T H Coffey
Private W Lea

Gloucestershire Regiment

Lieutenant John Peate

Hampshire Regiment

Private A J Veale
Private H Berkeley Benyon

South Lancashire Regiment

Private George Morgan
Private Arthur J Ormond

Welch Regiment

Captain E H Westby
Sergeant T M Davies
Sergeant E Prichard
Sergeant W C Sudds
Private C Bickerstaffe
Private John R Carne
Private Robert Davies
Private Gilbert Davies
Private Alfred W Forsyth
Private Richard Goodridge
Private James Harries
Private John Harries
Private J F Rees
Private Evan Roblin
Private Hubert Smith
Private Gilbert J Smith
Private Warner

Sherwood Foresters

Private Frank Harries

Royal Berkshire Regiment

Company Quartermaster Sergeant G Y Allen

King's Own (Yorkshire Light Infantry)
Private Albert Wrenn

King's Shropshire Light Infantry
Private Joseph Davies
Private W Eden
Private Ernest A Gregory
Private Harold E Parcell

Middlesex Regiment
Private W Cornell

King's Royal Rifle Corps
Lieutenant George Huntington

Wiltshire Regiment
Sergeant A Glass
Sergeant E Kibblewhite
Sergeant H S Burton
Lance Corporal C Rand
Private D J Taylor

Manchester Regiment
Private G H Williams

York and Lancaster Regiment
Corporal William Way

Argyll and Sutherland Highlanders
Captain F J D Knowling MC

Royal Munster Fusiliers
Major F I Day
Lance Corporal W H Jones

Machine Gun Corps
Captain Ralph J Roberts
Private C F A Fordham
Private F T Jones

Labour Corps
Private Howard B Best

Royal Defence Corps
Corporal W G Mathias
Private W Pearce

Royal Army Service Corps
Private A Scott Lewis

Royal Army Medical Corps
Private C E Richards

Royal Army Ordnance Corps
Corporal James Murphy

Royal Army Pay Corps
Private Archie T W Jenkins

Royal Air Force
Lieutenant Colonel Leoline Jenkins DSO MC
Captain F Barclay
Second Lieutenant the Reverend J Wesley Howells

Canadian Expeditionary Force
Lieutenant John G Kenworthy *(16th Battalion)*
Sergeant G H Nicholls
Private William H Lloyd

Australian Expeditionary Force
Captain W H Nicholls
Private Ronald G Fishwick

96 A TENBY LIFEBOAT FAMILY

East African Mounted Rifles
Trooper E Lucien Laws

Indian Army
Lieutenant Colonel William Beadon *(51st Sikhs)*
Major J P May *(102nd King Edward's Own Bombay Grenadiers)*
Lieutenant J H L Walcott *(2nd Gurkhas)*

Died after discharge from effects of Service
Able-bodied Seaman T H Lillicrop *(Royal Navy)*
Private H L Bevan *(Pembroke Yeomanry)*
Company Sergeant Major J Rossiter *(Welch Regiment)*
Private G Mallin *(Welch Regiment)*
Private Ernest Powell *(Machine Gun Corps)*
Driver Joseph Rees *(Army Service Corps)*
Captain William Henry Thomas *(Royal Army Service Corps)*
Driver William George Rees *(Royal Army Service Corps)*

*(**Publisher's note**: Details of individual Servicemen and Servicewomen, including place of burial or memorial, can be found on the Internet at the Commonwealth War Graves Commission web-site at http://yard.ccta.gov.uk)*

PEMBROKE DOCK IN THE BLITZ

Pembroke Dock has a proud history, even within the last sixty years. It was to play a strategic role in the Second World War and suffer greatly as a result.

Home of the famous Sunderland Flying Boats based on the Milford Haven Waterway which helped enormously to win the War, as she fulfilled her role as no other could have done.

What a wondrous sight these high seaplanes looked, flying over and landing on the vast natural beauty of the Haven.

PEMBROKE DOCK IN THE BLITZ 97

They brought a sense of purpose and pride to the area, giving it something very unique for a small Welsh town; home of quite unassuming, caring, family people. They had to welcome many strangers. Servicemen, who would be billeted around the area. British, American, soldiers, airmen, Navy, pilots flying off around the world on dangerous missions and hopefully coming home to Pembroke Dock.

The expertise and bravery of the young men of the day in handling these highly innovative craft was amazing, and they loved them and every moment they spent on them.

Our flying heroes, honourable men, rising to the challenge to conquer the enemy and protect their fellowman by helping to win the War.

The maintenance crews working out on the water in all weather conditions to keep them going needed to be multi-skilled and stalwart.

It seems incredible that as we were in such close proximity to Pembroke Dock we had little comprehension of the effect of its suffering. Perhaps it was because we had no cars and seldom went out of Tenby. Or perhaps it was because adults didn't discuss certain matters in front of children. I don't know.

The Germans began their bombing campaign on Pembroke Dock in 1940 and at first the people were incredulous of what was happening to them.

They were to be subjected to many raids and learned first hand the full extent of War, when their relatives and friends were killed, injured and homeless as its result.

Falling bombs of all shapes and sizes: screaming bombs, parachute bombs, machine gun fire, fell all around and about them, destroying all in their path.

The townsmen looked for support in their time of desperate need and little seemed forthcoming. They felt they stood alone, unaided by the 'powers that be.' They were in a very vulnerable position with the docks, railway terminus, oil tanks, barracks, flying bases on water and land, armoury depot, fishing fleet. So many things the Germans would seek to bomb.

And yet they didn't seem to have even a modicum of defence. The siren didn't work. There were not enough air raid shelters and those they had were insubstantial. Constant battles with the hierarchy seemed to produce even more red tape and nothing else. They felt they stood alone.

Apart from the fear of being bombed in their beds, they had to live with the stressful feeling that things to protect them were not being handled well. They were naturally very frightened and had to be very brave. As one raid followed another, not just the 'Dock' but the villages around the nearby military airfield of Carew Aerodrome - Milton, Carew Cheriton, Carew itself - were all bombed.

The local Fire Brigade was marvellous. The Civil Defence and Home Guard, the Voluntary Services, all worked a twenty-four hour day to contend with the concentrated effect. The firemen were sometimes subjected to machine gun fire whilst they endeavoured to control the burning oil tanks. The appalling black smoke from which engulfed the town for days on end permeating everything. How were they to endure it?

None of their heroes of these events got any acclaim from people other than themselves. They scanned the papers for recognition of their valour and their plight and found next to nothing.

Hurt and demoralised, they decided they would have to help themselves. The siren still didn't work properly so townsmen took it in turns to stay up all night and raise the alarm.

Many of the older people moved out. Others felt they had to see it through and took shelter under the stairs, or even under a table, as their homes fell around them. It was almost impossible to continue their normal daily routine, getting the family to school and work. Sometimes they had water, sometimes not. They never knew after a raid if the shops they were registered with for their food would still be standing in the street. As many young family men were away at War, the women of the family had to be very strong, facing impossible situations on their own and often having elderly dependants and neighbours needing help nearby.

The human spirit rises to the occasion and help from kindly friends and neighbours was always forthcoming, as was the sharing of their scant food rations. It was a common sight to see one person or another going to one door or another for a cup of sugar or tea borrowed, until they got their rations, and then repaid.

Whilst reading about Pembroke Dock I came across this 'missive of coincidence':

Officers' Mess, British Army NAAFI, Palestine, May 1946: A German Lieutenant Colonel in his late thirties, standing at the NAAFI bar, introduced himself to a British Lieutenant Colonel, Tom Powell, REME, standing next to him, and offered to buy him a drink, which Tom accepted as the War had been over for a year.

In conversation Tom said: "I will be going home soon."

The German asked Tom: "Where do you come from?"

Tom replied: "Pembroke Dock."

The German officer said: "That is interesting!!! I led the attack on the oil tanks there in 1940 and left a big fire burning. Ah, time for dinner – will you join me?"

I did visit Pembroke Dock on one occasion as a small child. Wendy Nowell and I were about seven or eight. We had been picking 'milkmaids' up Jane Jenkins' field one summer morning and were walking home to dinner down the Upper Maudlins.

Wendy said: "I think I'll leave home this afternoon – I've got nine-pence in my money box."

"Oh!" I thought: "She's upset. Perhaps her dad is cross with her."

"All right" I said, "I'll ask my mother for nine-pence and come with you." I wasn't going to let her go alone.

I can remember saying to my mother in a very serious manner, "Mum, Wendy's leaving home this afternoon. Can I have nine-pence to go with her?"

I'm not sure what my mother thought of this; I could only ask because it was for someone else. Perhaps she thought she would teach this strange child of hers a lesson? Or perhaps she thought it as a cheap way of disposing of me? I don't know. But I got the nine-pence gas money without query, had my dinner and went to call for Wendy.

In Tenby all important journeys started at the railway station, another of our favourite haunts, as we often went in and sat by the fire on the big shiny leather seats in the waiting-room for a warm in winter. One of our schoolfriend's dad, Mr Daniels from Saint John's Hill, was one of the station-masters so he didn't chase us off.

We went to the ticket office and paid threepence each for two half-fare single tickets to Pembroke Dock. We knew the train couldn't go any further.

We were used to seeing trains, but this one was special. As soon as it stopped we were getting on it.

When the big train chugged in it sent out a loud hiss and a great cloud of smoke, engulfing the little foot-bridge. We hurried along the platform to find an empty carriage. It was the first time we had actually been on a train.

There was a deep gap between the platform and the little step of the carriage that we had to be careful of.

Once in we chose to sit on either side of the window which we pulled down by the big leather strap with buttonholes in it. These you pushed over a metal button to hold the window in the desired position, but it was very heavy so we did it together. The plush seats were comfy and we tried them as beds and knelt up on them to look at the pictures on the walls and examine the luggage-rack as we hadn't seen one of those before.

We found our train ride exciting and over too soon. Pembroke Dock Station. [Nowadays the railway line terminates in the town rather than at the docks.] Whistles blowing, flags waving as the train halted and we opened the door to get out. It seemed a long way down and we were a bit daunted by that gap, but the friendly porter gave us a hand.

The docks seemed large and awesome, full of naval vessels with big letters on them and high cranes loading goods on to them. We felt a bit frightened, as we had never seen a dockland before, so we headed for the town.

As the War had been in duration for about three years and Pembroke Dock had suffered badly from the bombing we were to see it at its worst.

The windows of the town's houses and shops were boarded up. Some property was razed to the ground and was a heap of rubble. Others were half-bombed; you could see half a bedroom with the curtains and bedding blowing in the breeze.

Interested in it all but not liking it very much as it wasn't as nice as Tenby. Wendy said: "I think I'll get my dad a present to take back out of my money."

"What does your dad like?" I said. Thinking of the only time we bought our dad a present at Christmas out of our Christmas carol singing money. We used to buy a stick of Erasmic shaving soap from Woolworths each year and our dad seemed to make them last. Razor blades were kept in a tin of Vaseline so that they lasted too.

We came to a fishmonger's. He had a display out front. Oh, kippers. My dad loves kippers. So in we went. Kippers were threepence a pair so the fishmonger told us, so we asked for one pair each for our dads' tea which he wrapped up in newspaper parcels.

Happy now with the thought of giving our dads a present, we spotted a double-decker bus with 'Tenby' on it so got on quickly to go home. All thoughts of running away forgotten.

Upstairs we scurried and sat in two seats so that we could both be by the window; the top of which was open, it being summer. We thought we'd stand up and wave to people as we went by. We were seldom on a bus, especially upstairs.

Waving our paper packages out of the window mine got caught on the branch of a tree and I lost dad's kippers to the birds. But my friend Wendy shared hers with me, one each in half a piece of newspaper.

PEMBROKE DOCK ROLL OF HONOUR

(Published with permission by the author from Pembroke Dock Town Council)

WORLD WAR II

Servicemen killed in Action

Sergeant A W Allen	Army
Lieutenant Quartermaster W L Ambrose	Essex Regiment
Sergeant Pilot J H Bevans	RAF
Bombardier B Beasant	Royal Artillery
Private K L Bittle	Royal Marine Engineers
Private R F Bittle	Royal Army Ordnance Corps
Captain Quartermaster W Cooper	Welch Regiment
Private M C Clapton	Airborne Forces
Private E R Darlington	2nd Battalion Yorks
Sergeant D J Davies	Signals
Sergeant E Davies	Army
Private T A Dilworth	2nd Buffs
Lance Sergeant E C Donohoe	King's Shropshire Light Infantry
Sapper E C Edwards	Royal Engineers
W G Evans	Royal Artillery
W R J Forward	HMS Glorious
Sergeant E George	Royal Engineers
Pilot Officer T J Hordley	RAF
Staff Sergeant C Isaacs	REME

PEMBROKE DOCK ROLL OF HONOUR

Chief Petty Officer A L James	*HMS Gloucester*
Sergeant R James	*Royal Tank Regiment*
Warrant Officer F E Johnson	*RAF*
Lieutenant C Kelly	*Royal Artillery*
Sergeant E G Lewis	*RAF*
Lance Bombardier G Lewis	*Royal Artillery*
Trooper A S Makin	*1st Tank Regiment*
Lieutenant G J Mathias	*Royal Navy*
Sergeant Engineer J McKenzie	*Royal Auxiliary Air Force*
P McGrath	*RAF*
Gunner A J Morris	*Royal Artillery*
Sergeant Pilot J Mumford	*RAF*
N Owens	*RAF*
I Phillips	*Welsh Guards*
W A Phillips	*Royal Navy*
Sapper J S Power	*Royal Engineers*
Private R G Powell	*Dorsetshire Regiment*
Sergeant Pilot A Pricket	*RAF*
Chief Engine Room Artificer S J Pricket	*HMS Liverpool*
Sergeant M Rees	*RAF*
Lieutenant P Saunders	*Army*
Squadron Leader Reg H Thomas	*RAF*
Sergeant F Waite	*Canadian Tank Corps*
Pilot Officer E Williams	*RAF*

Merchant Navy

T H Hogg	*Merchant Navy*
1st Officer J Calnon	*Merchant Navy*
2nd Engineer W C Hare	*Merchant Navy*

Trawlermen

Third-hand Enginer D Evans	*Trawlerman*
Fireman J Evans	*Trawlerman*

Servicemen Missing - Presumed Dead

Sergeant C W Brinn	*Army*
Stoker D Broad	*HMS Exeter*
Gunner C G Brighty	*Royal Artillery*
Sergeant Observer C Catherall	*RAF*
Private I Cole	*King's Own Rifles*
Gunner F Dean	*Royal Artillery*
Ronald Davies	*HMS Hood*
Lance Corporal C W F Darbon	*Royal Army Ordnance Corps*
Sergeant N Earnshaw	*RAF*
Petty Officer G Gibby	*Royal Navy*
Private J Griffiths	*Army*
Private N H Griffiths	*Royal Artillery*
A B D Griffiths	

Pembroke Dock Air Raid Victims

S H Buxton	*Home Guard*
J A Bowen	*41 Laws Street*
Mrs A R Brizel	*6 Gwyther Street*
Miss K Brizel	*6 Gwyther Street*
J T Baskerville	*91 High Street*
Dorothy Dunn	*4 Gwyther Street*
Corporal Dunn	*4 Gwyther Street*
Agnes G D Evans	*37 Laws Street*
Mrs M E T Evans	*Prince Albert Inn*
Thomas Evans	*37 Laws Street*
Mrs H M R Hammerton	*35 Laws Street*
Mrs E J Harries	*35 Laws Street*
J F Harries	*35 Laws Street*
Mrs Maude Harvey	*16 Bush Street*
Mrs D Hearn	*6 Gwyther Street*
Mrs C E Heath	*3 Melville Street*
Maurice Heath	*3 Melville Street*
Mrs E Hutchings	*33 Laws Street*
Cyril M Jenkins	*Imble Lane*

PEMBROKE DOCK ROLL OF HONOUR 105

Arthur J Kavanagh *Air Raid Warden*	*Imble Lane*
Mrs C E Kinton	*14 Bush Street*
W H Kinton	*14 Bush Street*
David M Lenham *(18 months)*	*4 Gwyther Street*
Mrs E M Lenham	*4 Gwyther Street*
Alexandra McKenzie	*31 Laws Street*
Cyril McKenzie	*31 Laws Street*
Mrs L E McKenzie	*31 Laws Street*
Rhys Morris	*Pier Hotel*
Miss E Morris	*Pier Hotel*
Thomas Phillips	*Prince Albert Inn*
Walter S Pounder	*6 Gwyther Street*
Harry H R Reynolds	*39 Laws Street*
Mrs Elizabeth Reynolds	*39 Laws Street*
Henry Roach	*Prince Albert Inn*
Mrs A B Robinson	*4 Melville Street*
Mrs E F Saunders	*4 Tremeyrick Street*
J H Thomas	*31 Laws Street*
Elizabeth Williams	*Pier Hotel*
Matilde Williams	*91 Military Road*

Air Raid Victims Killed Elsewhere

Mrs M James	*London*	*26 Prospect Place*
C F Owen	*Gosport*	*43 Park Street*
Mrs Oakes	*London*	*Lewis Street*
Sidney Peters	*Plymouth*	*17 Brewery Street*
Mrs Sidney Peters	*Plymouth*	*17 Brewery Street*

*(**Publisher's note**: Details of individual Servicemen and Servicewomen, including place of burial or memorial, can be found on the Internet at the Commonwealth War Graves Commission web-site at http://yard.ccta.gov.uk)*

TENBY WOMEN AT WAR

In Tenby where we have so much to be proud of, the War years called on all our townsmen and women to step out of their normal routine and give of their time and energy to the joint cause.

A woman, in any generation, plays an exacting role. The needs of her husband, family and home have to have first priority in order for the family unit to run smoothly.

In the War they were asked to stretch their time and energy to join and run the various women's groups within the town and surrounding areas. Which they did, in an exemplary manner.

Right across the social spectrum, Tenby women responded. Rich worked alongside poor, and learned a respect and regard for one another that may not always have been there before, but was to continue for a lifetime afterwards.

Adversity brings out the best in kind people and, as they had a joint cause, there were no barriers.

One of our main essentials at all times is of course food. With rationing, supplying this was even more difficult than normal, and had to be strictly supervised to ensure fairness.

Lady Stella, Marchioness of Reading, who revived the **Women's Land Army**, was also the founder of the **Women's Voluntary Service (WVS)** in 1938. The organisation was formed with the Government's approval as they appreciated the great help that it would provide.

Our Tenby ladies proudly joined. Smart in their uniforms of grey-green tweed suits with maroon jerseys and felt hats, they had to pay for their uniforms themselves and worked hard to gain their medals, which they received for their achievements. Many of these ladies were middle-class and wouldn't normally have needed to work, especially in often very difficult, cold and dirty circumstances. But they fulfilled their roles of diverse duties to the highest possible standard. An example is the greatest teacher ... their team followed suit.

The British Restaurant in Central Hall, Lower Frog Street [now Tenby Royal British Legion] was opened up and run by these ladies. Many people who wouldn't have had a meal otherwise could afford to eat there at very low cost. Soup was one-penny; dinner of meat and vegetables was sixpence. Pudding was two-pence, and tea a penny.

We children, on the rare occasions that we ate there thought it was lovely, like a big party. Lots of local people of all ages and Servicemen, sitting down together to have a meal. As so little food was available for anyone at home people were hungry most of the time and this helped to eke out the rations. We never had money for more than soup or pudding, but it was a little treat to eat out with our friends. I shall always remember the smell of these dinners; the mixture of savoury and sweet food in a large quantity was unlike any we encountered elsewhere.

The adults had the company and the moral support of their friends and neighbours. They were able to discuss their problems and exchange views on the War's progress. Gentlemen living alone could enjoy a nice cooked meal, with no washing-up afterwards.

Some women found their voluntary work very rewarding. Loved ones being away at War and the constant worry that they had to live with, keeping busy, doing things for other people, gave them a sense of purpose and took their minds off their own problems. So tired at the end of the day, they readily fell asleep, which was a blessing for the mind and body. The War was an endurance test for everyone which lasted six years and coping with it on a daily basis became routine. Those so deeply involved hardly noticed the difference it made on their lives.

Of equal importance to the food, the WVS provided support and comfort, often begged or borrowed from their own, or friends', scant rations. The very way in which it was provided gave moral support to their fellow Civil Defence Workers.

Always on site in any emergency situation, outdoors in all weather and War conditions, their emergency facilities gave hot drinks to the Air Raid Wardens, the Bomb Disposal Unit, the Fire Service, the Ambulance Services as well as the victims. As they were on the spot so to speak, they were the first to offer some relief and warmth. Blankets were readily available as our townsmen had kindly donated any they had to spare, any other voluntary workers or householders who were short of vital equipment, or had surplus items, could contact the WVS to help. In Tenby they used the Town and Visitors' Club [at Laston House in Castle Square] and the Council School for their training and meetings.

As Tenby's population increased by about one thousand at the time, due to the influx of military personnel and to the homeless people coming to us for sanctuary, many from Swansea where they had been badly bombed due to the docks, but also from as far away as London, accommodation had to be found for them. A Billeting Officer was appointed.

The WVS worked with him finding 'billets,' as their temporary accommodation was called. Most of their requests for homes for evacuees were generously forthcoming. Not easy for anyone, at any time to have strangers in their homes. Many already had big families of their own and their men had gone to War. A lot were single parents. Not easy for those seeking shelter either. They were completely lost, separated from their loved ones and home and treasured possessions. Any new world is frightening to a small child, even one as beautiful as Tenby until adjustments were made. A lot of kind help was necessary.

The problems that the War imposed, just on the essentials of every day life were countless and varied. Apart from food in our bellies and a roof over our heads, we of course needed clothes on our backs. Vanity was to quite an extent a thing of the past. Economy, mend and make-do became the words of the day. Nothing was cast aside. Wastefulness was wickedness. Items no longer needed were past on to other family or neighbours with goodwill. Trousers were patched, as neatly as possible. Some became positive works of art. Socks were patiently darned. Sometimes more darn than sock. Garments were unpicked and used the other way round. Adults' clothes were cut down and made into children's. In our big family we had many such garments and were glad of the warmth that they provided. A mother needed her ingenuity to clothe a family on next to nothing. As a big family we had plenty of clothing coupons, but they were no help when you didn't have the money to spend them with. They were often sold to our better off neighbours, but the essential food or shoes were the priority for the money.

[Purchase of items of food and clothing during the War required 'points' from a ration book plus money for the required expenditure - sale of surplus 'points,' perhaps due to insufficient finances, was strictly speaking illegal and part of what was known as the 'black market.']

In Tenby the WVS set up a Clothes Exchange Shop, just past Woolworths in Tudor Square. I shall never forget one painful day when I had been sent to partake of this charitable service. There is nothing in life that hurts your pride so much as a child than to have to ask for charity. I had been sent to take an item of clothing and ask for a new coat. I was very loath to do this, but too strictly brought up to refuse. I suppose I was about six, and I went on my own just before lunch-time. It was blowing a gale and I was so small I could hardly stand against it, but still I couldn't pluck up the courage to go into the shop. People came and went and I stood outside getting more wet and bedraggled.

Then just as the lady came to turn the sign on the door from 'open' to 'closed,' I shot in. I will always remember her kind smile when I handed her my sodden paper carrier-bag and said, "Mummy said, could I have a new coat please?" She lifted me onto a table, took off my wet shabby coat and from the clothes rack found me a neat little green coat; it only needed a button on the belt. I was so thrilled and wondered why it had taken me so long to go into the shop. Just one example of the role these kind ladies played in our lives, and how much harder it would have been without them.

The WVS set up an unofficial Tenby Housewives Service in common with other towns across the country, to provide help to others on their own doorstep. Neighbours soon got to know who were their WVS ladies and could seek their help with their daily problems. If she couldn't solve them herself at least she knew where they could go for help. Everyone was dealing with things they had not experienced before and guidance was necessary at times.

So many small things are paramount in War. They had to keep a check of the number of people in any one area at any one time, as in the event of a bombing the Air Raid Wardens would need to know how many were safe or missing. Women were able to fill this role, each within their own area.

In Tenby we eventually had quite a lot of children evacuees. Finding them temporary homes was an important role for the WVS. Many of our notable townsmen were generous enough to provide them with one. Sometimes taking more than one child as no one liked to split family members unless it just couldn't be helped. Many also went to more humble homes and sometimes became lifelong friends.

They attended our school. One little fair-haired girl was so talented. To our delight our teacher, Mrs Wright, often asked her to sing and dance for us, which was an entertaining change from lessons. One boy who was a handful often stole from his mother's purse before coming to school. She didn't let him get away with it and went to our headmaster, Ossie Morgan, who came with her to our class where the boy was searched in front of everyone until the money was found. Sometimes in his shoe. He then took him to his study for the cane. An important lesson was of course learned by us children from this type of episode but it gave us an awful feeling. We were so sorry for his little mother. His father was away at War.

Even when the War ended, the WVS still had a very important role to play for many years to come. Plenty of our townsmen and women were still in need of help with food and clothes and ancillary equipment. Stockpiles in various church halls had to be checked and redistributed. Rationing went on for many years so supplements were still necessary. There was a special type of milk powder that was available for mothers who couldn't breast-feed their babies and they continued to supply this. Also they supplied concentrated orange juice and cod liver oil for young children to ensure healthy growth on a meagre diet.

They organised the victory celebrations, street parties, dances and other events. Many themselves with sad hearts as they had perhaps lost loved ones during the War. But there was no time for self-pity. Everyone had their own sadness to bear. Life must go on with renewed vigour as our War heroes coming home were entitled to all the help that could be given to them in order for them to readjust to daily lives as civilians after six years of War.

They still had to find jobs and homes within their own small home town and often resentment set in. As our heroes looked for help after giving their all and found, due to red tape, it wasn't always forthcoming. Many frustrations and social problems existed and no one was experienced in dealing with them.

The WVS acted as an important buffer between the needy and authority, trying always to act with kindness, understanding and impartiality.

I follow with an aside about two of our dear Tenby ladies of whom I possess a photograph of them proudly wearing their WVS uniforms and newly presented Long Service Medals during the War.

One is Mrs Hilda Lewis, 9 the Flats, Bridge Street, Tenby, wife of Tenby Lifeboatman Bertie Lewis and beloved aunt of Freddie Lewis, also a Tenby Lifeboatman, of Heywood Court, Tenby; Freddie is now 75 years old and the dearest man.

The other is Mrs Margaret (née Brooking) Glass of 12 the Flats, Bridge Street, Tenby. Beloved aunt of my school friend Margaret (née Warner) King. Margaret, like myself, is now 64 [1999] and she has been next door neighbour and kind friend to Freddie Lewis all her life, both on the Quay and at Heywood Court.

During the War, these ladies working with the WVS paid special attention to all the elderly people in the town, paying regular home visits to provide for their needs and to ensure their safety.

Sadly these ladies have now passed away but their memory is still with their friends and loved ones. I myself knew Hilda Lewis, who was like an aunt to my sisters and myself.

I have composed a poem *Call my name, my dear* for all those who have known the sadness of losing a friend and loved one [published on the opposite page].

Mrs Margaret Glass was a notable lady of our Tenby town. Her work with the Tenby WVS brought her in touch with many eminent people who were associated with the Services.

One outstanding event in her diary [1960] was when she was invited to attend the wedding of Mr David Hicks and Lady Pamela Mountbatten at Romsey Abbey in Hampshire.

She was amongst a thousand guests and noted that although it was snowing hard the roads to the Abbey were lined with people, several deep; some holding hot-water bottles. The inside of Romsey Abbey was decorated totally in white. The bride, of course, looked really beautiful. There were so many guests at the reception that it had to be held in two rooms: one at the Mountbatten's home of Broadlands for the principal guests; the other in a hall on the estate. The wedding cake stood on a dais in the hall. It was cut by the

Call my name, my dear

by

Avis Nixon (née Cottam)

(Dedicated to all those who have known the sadness of losing a friend and loved one)

I thought I heard you call my name
Softly on the breeze, it came.
Whispering through the leaves of trees,
Along the tide-line of the shore,
I stood alert and heard no more.

Why do I hear, now you have gone,
Your words sweet, as in a song?
They call with love, as once you did,
And teardrops form, on my eyelid.

My heart wells up, to catch your love,
Does it come on the wings, of the sweet white Dove?
Does it shine in the dew of the wild white rose?
I look and listen, here and there.

This deep gap, so hard to bear,
It helps a lot, if I can hear,
You call my name, my dear.

bridal couple and distributed among the guests, who drank the newly-weds' health in champagne. Mr and Mrs Hicks then shook hands with everyone, including Mrs Glass who had not previously met Lady Pamela; Mrs Glass said she was absolutely charming and that she wouldn't have missed the occasion for anything. Quite unexpectedly, she was then invited to visit Mr Hicks' mother and stay at her London home.

This indomitable Tenby lady, Mrs Margaret Glass, and her great friend, Miss Joan Ridpath, founded the Joans' Club [1947] at Rest Harrow in Cresswell Street. There they were joined by other Tenby lady friends: Mrs Esther Morgan, Mrs Hilda Lewis, Mrs Fanny Davies and Miss Maud Simpson. Mrs Glass was an excellent cook and made all the cakes for the club. When in later years a new community centre was built in Augustus Place [in 1961 by Tenby Rotary Club with furniture from Tenby Round Table] the Joans' Club moved there. As the older members passed away, new ones joined and the Joans' Club is still going strong in Tenby today.

Another notable townswoman with Tenby WVS was Mrs Emma Elizabeth Diamond who lived at 'Sandwich' in Park Terrace. She was asked to appear on television [mid-1950s] in a programme, watched by 750,000 viewers, entitled 'Life begins at 80.' This lady, as all who knew her would confirm, was a very young and active 80. She was selected, after a search by the old independent Welsh television station TWW, for young at heart 80s; her nomination being by the WVS who had forwarded a list of candidates to TWW headquarters at Cardiff.

Within a few days of receiving this list TWW sent producer Anthony Holyland to interview Mrs Diamond at her home. The programme was broadcast on a Monday evening at 7 pm and on the panel with Mrs Diamond were Ada Reeve, the old music hall star, and as a special guest Major John Francis of Carmarthen. Mrs Diamond had received long lists from TWW about what she should and should not wear on TV.

TENBY WOMEN AT WAR 115

An indomitable lady, she would always be herself. She readily answered their personal questions, about what her wedding dress was like and what was her favourite food, she replied 'steak and kidney pudding.' She had travelled to Cardiff accompanied by her WVS friend Mrs Glass and they stayed at the Llandaff Hotel.

Mrs Diamond had come to Tenby from Sandwich in Kent, hence the name of her house, in April 1923. Following serving in the Royal Marines, Mr Diamond had been a coastguard there and carried on as one in Tenby until 1953. Mr and Mrs Diamond had a family of two daughters, one son and three grandchildren. Their son Frederick Charles, like his father, joined the Royal Marines and served on the *Indomitable* in the War.

The conscription of women into the forces began in December 1941. The National Service Act (Number 2) applied to women between twenty and thirty years. In 1942 the age limit was reduced to 19 years and in 1943 it was extended to fifty-one years.

Married women, not living apart from their husbands, were exempt as also were women with children under fourteen years of age.

Once conscripted, women could choose between the **Women's Royal Naval Service (WRNS - known as Wrens)** as my sister Joyce did, or the **Women's Auxiliary Territorial Service** or the **Women's Auxiliary Airforce (WAAF)**. If they did not want to join the Military Services their other options were in industry doing War work or munitions, as my eldest sister Dora did. Also they could join the Allied Services of the **Land Army** or the **NAAFI** which was the Serviceman's canteen service.

The proportion of women in the Forces or Allied Services, within the age-limits, was nine out of ten. Whichever their choice, they were to find themselves with a very different lifestyle. Those who opted for industry had to travel and live in industrial areas finding lodgings in private homes or women's hostels; often not very warm, comfortable or cheerful, after a hard day in a factory.

Men still working in industry were unused to women working next to them. Sometimes they resented them and were deliberately unhelpful. The women themselves had been used to lighter work and found it very hard on their bodies getting used to handling heavy tools and equipment. Still, everyone had to adjust. A lot of hurts had to be ignored as one tried to keep the objective in mind, regardless.

Women also found men made personal advances that were not always welcome. Many of them were married but their wives were away with evacuated children and they only saw them occasionally. But you don't have to have a personal relationship with a man just because you work with him, although you suffered anyway just because you were there.

Coming home for leave or the odd week's holiday was also a frustrating ordeal at times as trains could be hours late with no definite time of arrival and they just had to wait at the station, until they came in jam-packed and the journey had to be spent standing in the corridor or squatting on their baggage. The duration of their precious leave often dwindled en route. If they didn't get back at the appointed time it was a serious offence. It was not uncommon for them to have to go back a day or two after arrival.

With the social scale being so mixed during this time, only some of the girls came back to their home towns to live as many found their lifetime partners and married.

Those returning found jobs and housing at a premium. Although the War was over things were to be hard for a long time. Rationing went on until the early 1950s, as did shortages of furniture and other household and luxury items.

Those women who dutifully joined the Women's Military Services were to experience the greatest change of all in their lifestyle and, indeed, the greatest changes that they would encounter in all their lives.

First there was the strict military training. Learning to march and smartly represent their unit, getting used to wearing uniform, even including their underwear, was not easy. Living, sleeping and eating in barrack conditions with the same group of other young women with different personalities and behaviour habits, difficult at any time. But when nerves were taut and emotions often sad because they had lost loved ones, or family or romantic relationships had faltered it was very difficult indeed. Although on the other side of the coin, so to speak, it did ensure that no one suffered alone; there were plenty of supportive friends who made you laugh and kept you company.

This generation had been used to a strict upbringing, both at home and at school, but there was nothing to prepare them for the rigour of the training ground where you exercised until you dropped and were shouted at and ridiculed by your superiors even when doing your utmost. It didn't matter what you were good at, this was almost always ignored and you would be set to perform your duties at something completely different.

The roles within the Services were so diverse. A lot of women were given quite domestic duties being 'batmen' so to speak, to officers, looking after their every need, including their dress and diary, drinks and meals, then chauffeuring them to their appointments, valeting their car and performing maintenance work on it too.

Some acted as 'predictors' for anti-aircraft batteries, some went into planning, strategy, map-reading, monitoring battles on air, land, sea, on tabletop settings so that their superiors could see at a glance how things were progressing.

Some women drove trucks and jeeps and ambulances. Some were trained to use arms. Others went into the Special Branch and became undercover agents entering enemy territory to gain important intelligence. And then there were the Signal and Coding Units, very important in warfare. They were often at the 'front' in battle, along with our men.

Others just did simple office work as telephonists, typists and filing clerks or accounts' work. All equally vital as the Forces couldn't run without it.

The **Women's Land Army** had been introduced during the First World War, in order to leave fit and able men working on the land to be free to join the Armed Forces and serve their country.

In 1939 it was reformed and by 1941 the number of women serving was some 20,000. Eventually these numbers swelled to 80,000.

Many of the young women came from cities and were inexperienced in country life and animals. At this time most farm work was done by hand. Farms were smaller and farmers had little more than a plough with two cart-horses, or some, more wealthy, owned a tractor.

At harvest time the same reapers and binders went from farm to farm, hired for the occasion and often breaking down as they were so overworked. The same team of operators and Land Army girls went with them.

The Land Army girls were issued with a uniform, hard-wearing and suitable for the outdoor work that they were expected to do. Thick brown riding breeches, green jerseys, brown felt hats, khaki overcoats, leather boots and gaiters. Being female and without any daily discipline they adapted this to suit their taste and no two looked the same.

Treated as the poorer Service, so to speak, they were not allowed to use Servicemen's canteens like the NAAFI which seemed unfair. Also they were only allowed one week's holiday a year compared with twenty-eight days in the Women's Forces.

They received little or no travelling money and had to work where they were sent. Hardly worth going home for such a short time, their work became their life and many stayed on to become able farmer's wives when the War ended. If not 'living in' at the farm they would have to find hostel accommodation.

Their work was very hard and never done. They rose early for milking. When this was finished some Land Army girls delivered it around the local homes, shops, hotels and offices.

I used to go on the round with our Land Army girl sometimes from Watkins' Farm on the Narberth Road. She was such a pretty girl, happy and friendly. Sometimes she did the milk deliveries by horse and trap and sometimes in a small van. She used to go to the De Valence with my older sisters sometimes and if I was outside playing, she would take me for a ride. There wasn't much bottled milk then. The customer gave a jug and the milk was measured from the large metal churn into the correct measure. Two pints, one pint or half a pint. All this took time. Shops, cafes and hotels required larger quantities. By the time the milk round was complete it was nearly time to start milking again.

And then there was the cleaning, husbandry and harvest, sowing and planting.

You had to be strong and staunch to be a Land Army girl and you didn't always have the moral support of other girls to help you along. A lot of young women knew greater loneliness due to the isolation of the farms and the lack of other young people to befriend.

Even the people they were working for and trying so hard to help were sometimes suspicious of them as they were strangers in their homes.

Apart from the odd village hall dance or the radio which had to be used with economy, as it was invariably powered with a battery and had to be used with discrimination as you didn't want it to fade during the news' broadcast, there wasn't much to entertain them.

One of the highlights of the day was lunch-time when they sat down to their sandwiches or soup and listened to Workers' Playtime. This was a very popular radio variety show, broadcast each day from a different workplace canteen across the country. A spur to keep the munitions' workers happy it was a great training ground for our show business personalities who emerged to become famous. After it was finished you had the one o'clock news and then back to work. The majority of the country listened in this way and it was here that we learned all the popular songs and jokes that were part of our childhood.

If there was a dance or film show on in a nearby town that the Land Army girls wanted to go to, perhaps with a girlfriend from a neighbouring farm, they would walk the miles there or cadge a lift along the way. This method was repeated on the way home and often they sang as they walked along to keep themselves company. People sang a lot more in those days.

Sometimes in summer when we had the bedroom windows open we would hear their feet marching and voices singing as they came up the Maudlins back to camps or farms, getting back in the early hours only to know they had to get up early again at 5 or 6 am in order to do the milking.

Pressure was put on the farms to produce the maximum to feed the nation. So herds were larger as were flocks of sheep and litters of pigs, flocks of poultry and even rabbits. All were encouraged as part of the War effort and required looking after.

A strict check was kept on their numbers by the Ministry of Agriculture and no farmer was just allowed to slaughter animals for his own consumption. He could face a very heavy fine if found to have done so.

All this needed extra manpower when the only men left were too old or too young to go into the Forces.

Considering that they had to work so hard and were only given a second class rating, it was surprisingly popular as a choice with many adjustable young women of the day who didn't want to be stuck in factories day-in and day-out, or who didn't want the military regime of the Women's Forces.

With regard to the farmers slaughtering animals for their own consumption on the farm, it did go on illegally. Those who worked with the farmer and knew about it were given a share of the carcass. Even the pig's head was used to make brawn and fat was rendered out of the trimmings; all stored for another day.

The officials from the Ministry did spot checks and searched the farm premises when suspicious. Some very humorous subterfuge went on.

I can remember one farmer being caught unawares, so to speak, when the officials banged on the farm door late one night after he and his wife had gone to bed. He had a pig carcass hanging in the bathroom, it being the coldest place. He quickly put it in bed with his wife and covered it up before he went down to open the door. They never found it. Necessity is the mother of invention.

As animals gave birth at different times around the clock it was really an impossibility for the Ministry to keep an accurate check on the numbers at any one time, so the farmer had the advantage. Poultry, eggs and milk were also subject to doubt. No one honestly knew how many eggs their hens may lay each day or what exactly their milk yield may be.

As fresh eggs were very sought after and scarce we mostly used an awful yellow powered egg substance issued as part of our rations. Not bad in rock-cakes or other home baking, but the only way to serve it on the plate was as an omelette which was cooked in the frying pan and cut into triangles to share between the family. We ate it from necessity, not from any great desire. The same could be said for the margarine of the day which was commonly called 'axle grease.' As children we didn't have any jam for tea. We had a little sugar sprinkled on top of our bread and margarine to help it go down. We loved this, as it was so sweet and crunchy.

At the end of a hard day the Land Army girls often had a feeling of dead tiredness come over them and they went to their humble beds and sobbed themselves to sleep.

Homesick for their loved ones and the life they had enjoyed, but there were also times of extraordinary vitality, energy and determination which took over and helped them to carry on with their tasks.

There was no such thing as an easy life for anyone when we all had to unite to win the War.

The **Navy, Army and Air Force Institute (NAAFI)** was established on an international scale to provide our Servicemen and Servicewomen with canteen facilities wherever they may be posted.

Always run by British management, but often staffed with local people, it took a little bit of home comfort where there might not otherwise have been any.

Some of the women who were naturally domesticated felt that they could fulfil their national duty in this Service and the benefits that it provided were not to be underestimated.

The NAAFI Service provided a social canteen type club for Servicemen and Servicewomen.

They were set up in most towns and responded to the Serviceman's needs. Food, drink, cigarettes, sweets at a modest price in line with their pay.

Reading and writing rooms were available where they could find a little peace and quiet. Very necessary when you lived in a barracks with so many others.

Even if the Serviceman could not afford any other entertainment he could go to the NAAFI, get a meal and a drink and spend a convivial evening with friends playing cards, darts, dominoes or snooker and table tennis.

Our NAAFI workers in this Service played an invaluable role preparing, cooking and serving meals, cleaning tables and floors, washing-up dishes, acting as shopkeepers, barmaids, social friends and confidantes.

Because some of the NAAFI's were within their locality they could live at home. Others were expected to travel to distant parts in this country and around the world to provide NAAFI facilities.

As they were mixing with Servicemen on a very domestic and social level, many met their future husbands whilst providing this Service.

Considering that to quite an extent people often married quite impulsively, as their time together might be short-lived and they had to make the most of it while they had it, a great many marriages of the day lasted a lifetime. They were strong people because of what life had demanded of them and didn't give up easily in hardship. After the War they could face anything.

At the end of the War who could say how our family lives would have been if it had never happened?

There were to be many changes in our society as a result of it. No small community or indeed country could withstand such a major event and come out of it unchanged.

Those who did survive and came back to their loved ones found their attitudes changed by their experiences.

Some were more forceful and determined. Some sadly were infirm and shell-shocked.

The boys who had gone were now confident young men, hardly recognisable.

The girls who had joined up came back smart young women with minds of their own. Never to be totally dependent on their menfolk again.

Many were eager to marry their sweethearts and start family life. A new beginning. But of course housing was in short supply. People had been used to small incomes for so long, that a council house was their greatest hope. To attain this you had to go on a waiting list and live with your parents for up to three years.

This caused many family problems as different generations within the family found it difficult to cope with little or no space for personal privacy.

As the War effort had created full employment some found that suddenly they were out of work and many more like them were seeking jobs.

As the War work was a skill of its own it did not fit them for other trades. Many turned to building and decorating, plumbing and road work as new houses sprang up and others badly neglected during the War needed renovation. As did those large properties in Tenby town that had been requisitioned during the War.

No house looks quite the same when a small army has used it daily in their hobnail boots. Many were just skeletons of their former glory and needed a great deal of work and money spent on them.

As time passed many older people felt sad as they saw the standards and customs they had cherished in their lives spurned and diminished. Little qualities that added to the goodness of life in the War no longer seemed important in their present society. So much that they had enjoyed had not cost much money, but it gave more in thoughtfulness to others.

My friend Wendy reminded me of early on New Year's Day morning when people used to knock on the door of our house in the Maudlins with a cup for a coin (for Charity) and another cup of water with an evergreen twig. They brushed our palm to wish you a happy New Year. I had forgotten this as it is so easy to forget our old customs and sad to think that now many may be afraid to answer their own front door. We knew no such fear and it is the absolute freedom that we enjoyed that is our most treasured memory.

*(**Publisher's note:** The publisher's mother, Mrs Nesta (née Rowse) Fish, can remember another old Tenby New Year's Day custom, that of "First Foot In." Where by to bring good luck and prosperity it was required that the first person to cross the threshold of a house on New Year's Day was a dark-haired man; a service her father, Brixham fisherman Harry Rowse, performed for neighbours in Cresswell and Saint Mary's Streets.)*

VE DAY IN TENBY

After all the six years of fighting, the War in Europe ended and 8th May 1945 was declared Victory in Europe Day.

In Tenby we naturally joined in the celebrations, together with the rest of the Nation and our Allies. Every house, shop, street structure was resplendent with flags, banners, bunting and placards. Everything anyone could find in the attic, buy or make. Rations were being used up rapidly, to make cakes and jellies for street parties and welcome home celebrations, for our returning heroes.

What a wonderful parade we had in Tudor Square, with all the Servicemen and Servicewomen lined up on the roads and the local inhabitants, facing them on the pavement. Goodwill to all. We little ones were allowed the front row. The Service from Saint Mary's, our biggest Church, was broadcast through loudspeakers into the square.

Music was played after the Service, and on the Tuesday Winston Churchill's speech was listened to by everyone. We also had a very moving speech from King George VI. After the Thanksgiving the merriment began, everyone enjoying the moment, filled with joy and elation. The troops and airmen, locals, young and old dancing together in the streets.

The De Valence and every pub in town were packed to the door. It was the biggest party we children had ever seen, and we ran around the town, squeezing between the adults' legs to get to the next place. Lots of course we weren't allowed in.

An American Serviceman billeted by the South Beach in a hotel asked us into the kitchen and gave us a sandwich each, which was a whole steak between two doorstep slices of bread. We ran off laughing, the most we aspired to at home was jam or meat-paste.

We listened for the sound of the Cadet Band. Where was it coming from? We tore off to join the procession with our huge bounty. Even the sun was shining. Up the Castle Hill we went. All the ships in the bay were dressed overall with flags. On the South Beach the assembly was unforgettable.

Hundreds of Servicemen and locals surrounding the band, with its kilted piper, all singing their hearts out, as only the Welsh can sing. In the evening there was an ENSA [Entertainments National Service Artists] concert at the De Valence for the adults, and bonfires were lit around the town for the first time since the black-out.

Tenby was at her most proud and united hour. An unforgettable day.

THEN FISH AND CHIPS AT FECCI'S

The De Valence Pavilion dance hall, was to play an important part in my family's life.

As the War had progressed, entertainment was sought by the many troops stationed around the area. In the villages of Penally, Carew, Saundersfoot, etc, we had airmen, soldiers of varying regiments, naval seamen and American forces. As Tenby was the 'star town' as you might say, those with leisure passes sought an evening's entertainment there.

A lot of them were billeted under canvas so some social life was essential. I'm not sure they all found comfort. I suppose that the officers did, as they frequented the more prominent hotels in the town, like the Royal Gate House, etc.

For the ordinary Serviceman on low pay it was a dance at the De Valence or a film at the Royal Playhouse or Shanly's South Beach Pavilion cinemas. Or a drink in one of the town's pubs that would be jammed packed from bar to door. Then fish and chips at Fecci's, similarly packed.

As little ones, dad occasionally sent us for fish and chips for supper. That was fish and chips for him, and three pennyworth of chips for each child. You can imagine us queuing with all the Army. It was one mad crush to the counter. A lot of the time treading on the well polished toecaps of their boots, until one took pity on us and held us up, so Mrs Fecci could see us and serve us.

Like most Italians the Fecci's loved children, however bedraggled, and when the chips were in the newspaper twist bags, she would scatter the fish batter crumbs all over the top so that we all had a few. We thought this lovely. The large parcel was nice and warming to our gloveless hands, so we made sure we took it in turns to carry it. There was usually a little hole somewhere, as we pinched the odd chip, but dad never mentioned it.

About a mile to walk home in the black-out, we sang all the way to keep ourselves company. Although very young we knew all the old Wartime songs - "I've got Sixpence," "Lily Marlene," etc.

The nights I like to remember are those when the moon lit our way, and we pointed out the various stars to one another. Wonderful minds children have, learning and teaching each other, without even realising it.

My elder sisters, in their teens to twenties, were able to go to the De Valence dances. Very attractive girls, they soon met partners who were to become husbands, and each marriage to last.

My mother in her early forties and still very attractive, obviously thought she was missing something of this gaiety, she joined them. I understand with my father's consent initially. I suppose he felt that she had been restricted a lot by the big family, low income and tied occupation. It was to be our downfall as a family, as she eventually met someone else and left us.

At school my sister Beryl was my protector against all adversity. A strongly built little girl with a mass of fair curls. She looked life in the face like a lion, and like a lion she was always hungry.

A born leader of other children, she was popular with her friends. She played with Billy and Ann Phillips in Heywood Lane a lot. They had a paddock at the back of their big house with ponies, Captain and White Flag. Both Beryl and my sister Barbara learned to ride.

They became so confident and Barbara loved animals especially. She could stand by a gate of a field, call the horse to her, mount and ride on it bareback. Mr Atwell, who had the stables in Upper Frog Street (opposite Tenby Market) used to hire out horses, both Barbara and Beryl rode these horses for him free to exercise them. I was far too frightened.

Sometimes three in a bed at night we would relate stories and poems to each other, as often we couldn't get to sleep. The houses of the Maudlins numbered one to thirty-six, we would name everyone who lived in each house, better than counting sheep, more interesting.

John and Tony Pilson, who shared our lives. Their parents who loved having us. I can remember sitting on an antique chaise longue while Mrs Pilson sang to us "The Teddy Bears Picnic." ... *If you go down to the woods today* ... Very apt, as we were seldom out of the woods. Their father must have wanted a little girl, as he used to sit me on his knee and rock me in the rocking chair. So much fond love we had from our neighbours. When we played 'kiss catch' in the road, Tony used to say: "Let me catch you Ava;" he was a year younger than me but thought I was his girlfriend.

As you can see what we lost in some ways, we made up for in others. As long as we came home at the appropriate time, we had a lot of freedom.

SCOTSBOROUGH HOUSE

One of the places we played in over the years was an exciting ruined castle in the Folly Woods off the road to Gumfreston.

It was a wonderful secret place for children. The tumble down walls and rooms with fireplaces and chimneys, became our imaginative homes, which we set out with furniture, made from arranged stones and wood.

It wasn't until an adult that I discovered the history of Scotsborough House and its significance to our town. I follow with a short account in case you too should be as ignorant as I. Its history as far as I know is uneventful. We were never taught about it at school.

In the early part of the 17th Century it was inhabited by Thomas ap Rhys. There is a large monument in Saint Mary's Church - blue and gold left of main altar - in memory of his beloved wife Margaretha. She died on the 1st May 1610 in childbirth with her tenth child in twelve years of marriage. She married at eighteen and died at thirty years of age.

She left a grieving family of husband Thomas and seven remaining children. Their figures are seen kneeling around her tomb. Thomas was devastated and he wrote her an epitaph:

> *I shall go to her*
> *She will not return home*
> *Let us go also*
> *And may we die with her*

Edward Llwyd, antiquarian and naturalist was a visitor to the mansion in 1697-8. Excavating in the grounds he found many fossils including nine flatfish skeletons and undescribed zoophytes (plantlike animals such as corals and sponges) thus proving that the sea had previously flowed up the Ritec Valley to the village of Saint Florence.

During his visit Llwyd complained that his letters were being intercepted and stolen by local people.

Jacobitism was then at its height, and plotting and intrigue were rife. This stranger was suspected by the locals as being a spy.

Scotsborough House was sold by the ap Rhys family in the 18th Century, and afterwards was allowed to fall into decay. All the stone work has disappeared. The remaining chimneys and huge ovens show it was erected when man's home also did duty as a castle and vice versa.

Wasn't it strange that we seven children, should come to play 'house' there some three hundred years hence?

I am grateful to the historians, but I don't agree that its history was uneventful, because it was not included in battles etc. Human stories are the most important part of our past, and we are proud to have shared in a small way.

MY BEST FRIEND WAS WENDY

My best friend was Wendy Nowell, she lived in the Maudlins and was the same age as me. We spent many childhood hours together, compatible and imaginative, our games were like stage plays. We the actors went from scene to scene, if other children joined in they were given parts but mostly we played all the roles.

One concert party we put on in her dad's pigeon shed, at the top of her garden, involved dressing up in some long dresses and hair ornaments. We had rigged up a curtain held on to a shelf with some of her father's heavy tools. We had decided which songs we should sing. Wendy has a beautiful voice. I was about to make my grand entrance from behind the curtain to sing "My Sweet Little Alice Blue Gown," when I trod on the edge of the curtain and a chisel fell off the shelf and stuck in my scalp.

My friend examined it and said: "You're bleeding, you'll die."

I had to get home to dad, he was our only doctor. I've often laughed to myself when I've thought how funny we must have looked, in our dressing up clothes and far too big high heels, running up the hill home with me holding my head and crying: "Dad! I'm dying!"

Wendy's father also kept greyhounds, Flash and Tina. It was our job to exercise them, and being only seven or eight and both small and thin, they were bigger than us, but we did it in a professional manner. No running off to play with them. We mostly went up the Narberth Road and through the three fields that are Upper Hill Park now.

To us it was a well-trod path to Waterwynch, about three miles from home. One cottage we went past had an old gentleman with a white beard like Father Christmas, who used to sit on a chair by the gate in summer. Sometimes if lucky we were told to take sixpence and a jug for his home-made ginger beer.

It was quite a job carrying it home without spilling it. We kept having sips, we hoped wouldn't be noticed, so the level went down a bit.

Always on the look out for some new interest. We became Busy Bees (chief ones of the group) born managers but not bossy so all followed, hopefully. This was a children's group of helpers for the People's Dispensary for Sick Animals (PDSA).

Ours was run by Miss Audrey Hand, who lived with her parents and two sisters around the Serpentine Road. We were in awe of her sisters, elder pupils at the Greenhill Grammar School [now the public library and further education centre] in Greenhill Road opposite the then Council School. Top scholars, violinists. Audrey unfortunately suffered from epilepsy, although at such a young age we didn't really realise what was wrong with her. We were kind and compassionate towards her, we thought it was nice that we had an adult friend. She was very tall I remember, I suppose in her twenties. We just used to call and ask if she was coming out to play. She enjoyed our company, as usual our imaginations ran riot. We ended up in her mother's sitting-room one day, Audrey on the piano, me screeching away on the violin, and Wendy singing sweetly. Unfortunately, her mother came in and we were ushered out.

On one occasion Miss Hand and I went for a walk in the Folly Woods. I had a job keeping up with her long strides, and we conversed on various subjects, both of us were interested in Literature (composition and poetry) - new to me at that age. We had walked about two miles and were sitting on the banks of a stream near a tumble down house.

Previously, Wendy and I had made our own little table in the centre from stones and Welsh slate. A jam jar of dying wild flowers in the centre. In our minds we were leaving it nice, as a surprise for a tramp who might want to spend the night there.

I had wanted to show it to Miss Hand, and we were talking about the Wood Anemones that were in flower, and she told me that she had written a poem about them and it had been published in a newspaper. I said: "Did you Miss Hand?" And all of a sudden she clutched her head, and her face contorted, and she fell sideways into the water.

I knew I had to get her face out in case she drowned, so I pulled her head up the bank. I was very frightened as we were in a lonely spot. I knew there was a farm-worker's cottage, that we had passed in the lane on the way down. A young lady with a lovely dark-haired baby lived there.

Messages shooting to my brain. I must go there for help, my breath was causing pains in my chest as I pounded up the stony path. I must get help. What if the lady isn't in? Where is the next house? Oh, a good way up on the main road.

When I reached the cottage gate it was locked, but I could see the front door was open and the pram on the lawn. So I climbed up the bank and over the top, risking being thought downright cheeky, as the emergency demanded of me. I knocked hard on the door and the young lady came down the passage. I was panting and very hot. I said: "Please excuse me, can you help? A lady has fainted down in the woods, by the stream. Could you bring a cup of water? She's too big for me to lift."

I could see I had panicked her, but she fetched a cup, and lifted the baby from the pram, and we scurried back down to the wood me explaining as we went. That Miss Hand was

MY BEST FRIEND WAS WENDY 133

like a schoolteacher, but she had something wrong with her head, and sometimes had fits.

When we got to the river bank Miss Hand had just come round on her own, as she had risen and was staggering towards us. We walked back up the path together, thanking the lady, and then the two of us walked the miles home. She had brought a bag of sweets which we shared as we went along, and I daringly held her hand.

After I told my sisters about my little adventure, they suggested that we should go to the Folly and thank the lady properly. So Wendy, Beryl and I walked out one evening, with whatever little things we could find to take as gifts for the baby and the pretty lady.

She was pleased to see us, as she was lonely, her husband was a cowman to the Cornish Down Farm which had a valuable herd of Jerseys. He worked long hours, and as she was from Carmarthen she did not have any relatives nearby. My elder sisters befriended Mrs Davies for her time in Tenby. Took the baby out for walks. When eventually Barbara had a son of her own, she called him Daryll after the lovely baby.

One of our near neighbours and friends was Gwyneth Bryn. An only girl with two brothers Dezzy and Ronnie, she kept friends with my elder sisters Dora and Joyce. To this day she is still friends with them.

She married before the end of the War Fred Brenchley, who was brought up by the Fecci's. I can remember on one occasion, being told quite urgently to go and tell Fred Brenchley that he was wanted on the phone from the hospital. We knew Gwyneth had gone into hospital to have a baby. This was unusual because most babies were born at home, with the help of our local midwife. Sometimes my mother was also called in to help, and strangely she was good at this, although I can never remember her nursing us.

Fred came striding over and took the stairs two at a time to the phone on the landing. We all waited anxiously at the bottom. He came down with a big smile on his face, sat on the bottom stair and said Gwyneth has had a baby girl. As we were congratulating him the phone went again, Fred flew back up. Down he came, sat down and said Gwyneth had had another baby girl. Poor Fred, we little ones were still expectant of another ring. He had survived the War and never been so stunned.

Old Mrs Bryn was a very caring mother, and rallied round to help all she could. Gwyneth and Fred set up home in a prefab in Heywood Court at the end of mam's garden. A number had been built for demobbed Ex-Servicemen and their families on the Tennis Courts off Heywood Lane. [The publisher was born at number thirty-nine in 1953, the prefabs were demolished in 1965 and replaced with flats and pensioners' bungalows.]

My sister Beryl and I used to call to take the twins Rosamund and Maxine for a walk in their pram. The procedure for this outing was lengthy, as the two babies had to be got ready to pristine standard. When Gwyneth wasn't coping too well with this new demanding role, she stood at the fence and yelled: "Mam!" And mam came flying, little legs waving behind her, up the path to help. I can remember thinking how nice it must be to have a mum who came when you called.

When the dark-haired babies were bedecked with their bonnets of pleated ribbon and white swansdown, we took off to give the mum a breather. What a strange entourage we must have looked, as Beryl and I would have only been half clean and tidy, scruffy plimsolls on our brown feet. We seldom owned socks even in winter. Our crowning glory of thick curly hair was only washed once a week in rainwater and was often tangled and untidy.

Still we were known to have common sense and be trustworthy. Beryl the tomboy, was also a born mother and she always had someone's child to care for. I just went along for the company. The babies' pram was very high, black, with a hood either end. We were hard put to see over the top with the hoods up, so had to peer round the sides as we went along for any obstacles. As Tenby is all hills, we were not sure which was the easiest, going up or coming down. Going up we had to stretch our little bodies out with our bottoms in the air, and coming down we had to keep one foot on the brake, so it didn't run away with us. Still it was worth it, for the times we were stopped and the lovely babies admired.

Some thirty odd years later when I had my shop in Milford Haven, Fred called and I was showing him my husband's workshop, and he leaned and kissed me on the cheek and said: "That's from Gwyneth to an old friend."

I didn't know until later. It was a goodbye kiss, as he died of cancer, and left his affairs in order. He knew he was going. I can still cry about it. With his cafe on the North Beach, and his membership in the Rotary Club, he was a notable, kind and respected sociable man, an asset to Tenby.

It was a Sunday morning when we children first met Mrs Gibbons. We were stretching out over a bridge on the Marsh Road, trying to reach some Pussy Willows to take to school on Monday. Our cotton dresses were tucked into our navy school knickers so as not to impair us.

We were obviously engrossed entirely in our efforts, as small children are, and oblivious of our appearance. When a gentle voice said: "Good morning children." We turned aghast certain we had been found doing something wrong. "Would you like the help of my stick to get your willows?"

We looked with round-eyed surprise, at this elegant elderly lady standing beside us. Her hair was silver and pressed into soft waves down her face, which was also soft and peach coloured, her blue eyes were smiling, on her hands were beautiful rings. We stared as only children stare, and she gave us a knowing smile and handed us her silver topped stick to reach the branches. We picked our willows with embarrassed haste, and handed it back hoping we hadn't dirtied it, and straightened our dresses.

"Which way are you going home children?"

"Up the Heywood Lane Miss," I said.

"Well that's splendid we can walk together. Would you like that?"

"Yes thank you Miss." Although young we were aware we were in rather strange company.

My sister Beryl had a three-corner tear in her dress and walked over on her shoes, which made them look even worse. Wendy was rather tidier than us. Mrs Gibbons held my hand and I held Wendy's. Beryl trudged along with the willows, kicking the 'dock leaves' on the verge, and answering Mrs Gibbons' questions.

"Do you children go to Church on Sundays?"

"Sometimes we go to Sunday School Miss."

"Which one do you go to?"

"Anyone our friends are going to Miss, but we were christened Church of England."

"Only I was christened in a Catholic Church as the Nuns helped my mother when I was born, as our dad was away at sea."

"Is your father in the Navy then?"

"No Miss he is the Lifeboat Mechanic in Tenby, and he's got a Certificate in a Gold frame on our landing."

"You have a brave and interesting father don't you?"

"He's very strict he is Miss, he gives us the strap if we're naughty."

Mrs Gibbons paused and leaned on her stick: "Well children this is where I live." We looked up, Heywood Lodge was written on the gatepost. "Would you like to call and see me this evening, say six o'clock, you can bring any of your little friends."

"Thank you very much Miss."

We skipped off chattering like three monkeys. To think we had been invited to a rich lady's house. We ran home for our

Sunday dinner. A roast joint which father carved and Yorkshire puddings and roast potatoes.

In the afternoon we decided to tell our friends and neighbours John and Tony Pilson, about our new friend, and how they could come to her house with us if they behaved themselves, we would call for them at a quarter to six and they would have to comb their hair, as it was a posh house.

Just before six o'clock we nervously entered the gateway of Heywood Lodge, a wide and curving gravel driveway led to the front door of a large country house. The outer door was white with half glass, and a brass bell handle which said 'pull.' John Pilson didn't need telling twice, and we all giggled when it rang. Gazing through the glass and through that of a second door, we saw a maid in a black dress and frilly cap and apron hurrying through the hall, she opened the door to us: "Come in children, Mrs Gibbons is expecting you."

We walked across the lovely wide hallway and were shown into a beautiful sitting-room furnished with antique furniture, and deep sofas covered with rose patterned fabric. French windows led out to the garden. Mrs Gibbons rose and told us to sit. The large sofa behind me seemed rather high and as I knew I mustn't climb, I did a sort of backward jump and landed on the big down cushion with a big 'puff' which seemed to amuse Mrs Gibbons.

She said: "You know children whether you go to Church on Sundays or not we are supposed to say Prayers to God, to thank him for his blessings, for the woods you play in, for those willows you picked." We sat like little pupils very serious. "Well if I read a little Prayer to you," she said getting a small book out of a cupboard, "Will you sing a little hymn for me?"

"Yes Miss."

"All Things Bright and Beautiful."

When we had finished we each received a sweet from a jar in the cupboard, and then we went into the wonderful garden.

Walkways with small box hedges, we used to leapfrog over, our gracious lady included. High conifers we used for 'hide and seek,' Mrs Gibbons joined in. Golf balls were hit and missed on the bottom links, shared with the garden of Gwilym Lloyd George (the local MP and son of Prime Minister David Lloyd George, he later became Lord Tenby). How fortunate we were, this dear lady came to all our little sales, to raise money for PDSA. Dug her beautiful ringed hands into tubs of sand, for a lucky dip. Watched our little plays and concerts that Wendy and I made up. She meant so much in our lives. During the War she had evacuees in her home to stay. Lovely lady of our town.

SHANLY'S SOUTH BEACH PAVILION

The side of the road opposite our side known as Broadwell Hayes has a different name, the Maudlins, and numbers one to thirty-six had recently been built. Semi-detached council houses with gardens to the front and back. They housed many young Tenby families. Some with nearly as many children as us. Our children were soon to make friends with theirs, and in some cases these friendships have lasted a lifetime.

Never can I remember any anti-feeling against our family, because they were not Tenby people so to speak. I don't think there was a house in the road that we hadn't been in at some time and that included the Upper Maudlins of privately owned houses and around the Serpentine. Indeed, we were especially asked to join mealtimes on occasions to set an example in manners to their children. As we played with their children we were invited by Mr and Mrs Groom who had a business in town and Mr and Mrs Morgan, known as 'Morgan's the Chemist.' When Wendy Nowell and I spoke of our friends and neighbours we could relate the names of every person in every house from the bottom of the road to the top.

SHANLY'S SOUTH BEACH PAVILION

In a small town people naturally have to harbour their privacy to some extent, as they are more immediately affected by their neighbour's opinion than people living in a more highly populated area.

At the same time as people had no wish to pry, they had a concern and compassion for their neighbours. Once the War started they were all affected in the same way, and the mutual regard showed in an inter-sharing of things in short supply. Very few people owned a refrigerator and any perishable commodity was shared with neighbours. They in turn sent you garden produce at harvest time. Clamps, earth storage for root vegetables, were made in the garden. Beans were salted and put down. The housewife of the day was multi-skilled as she bottled and preserved everything at her disposal.

Even eggs were put down in an earthenware crock using a product called Ising Glass. It was a fluid solution in which eggs floated. The shells suffered somewhat and they went powdery. Once the eggs were broke into a frying-pan they really bubbled up and spat at you. Throughout the War eggs were scarce as they were essential for baking and fetched a high price on the 'black market' for those who could afford them. I can remember taking a dozen to a lady for the farmer. The eggs were still smeared with chicken dirt and feathers to show that they were fresh. Each egg was wrapped in newspaper and they were packed in a box. I was told to collect seven-shillings and sixpence. At this time many people lived on five-pounds a week.

In a seaside town like Tenby people often move there to retire and when one or the other loses their lifetime partner there is a big gap. Few people used cars, even if they owned them as the petrol allowed to ordinary people was very scant and had to be kept for emergencies. We were often asked by older ladies to fetch their shopping. 'Going messages' as we called it.

This was quite involved in the War years as each person had to register with one particular grocer and butcher in town in order to get their rations. The shopkeeper was only allowed his quota according to the number of customers on his books. We had to take and look after their precious ration books as well as their money and shopping list. Queues at every shop, as it took extra time for the shopkeeper to cut the coupons out and stamp the books. Also at this time so many products were not pre-wrapped and butter, cheese, sugar, tea were all cut and weighed at time of purchase. Even bread and shop cakes were put on the scales and weighed to ensure you didn't have more than you were entitled to.

Greengrocery and fish were not rationed in the true sense, but as these were also scarce it amounted to the same, and when tomatoes or fruit came into the shop, a long queue formed and each person could have a pound until they were gone. Often you queued for nothing. For 'going messages' we usually received threepence. This was the brass hexagonal coin of the day which we loved as it was easy to handle and not easy to lose.

My mother never suggested taking this money from us. I suppose she felt it was a form of behaviour training. We then had our own pennies to go to the pictures which we had earned.

Lucky as we were for a small town, we had two cinemas. The Royal Playhouse in White Lion Street, nearly the same as it is today, and Shanly's South Beach Pavilion which to us seemed very special. Down the 'grand staircase' of wide concrete steps to the foyer. Still there in the cliff-side but overgrown to some extent now - Shanly's as we called it was demolished in 1981.

We paid our threepence at a kiosk in the foyer and were allowed into the wide corridor with full glass windows either side to enable you to see the beautiful views of the beach, the sand dunes, Caldey and Giltar Point. You felt as if you were going to walk out over the sea.

The decor of the cinema was very *art nouveau*. The floor and walls were cream and green, and to the right of you were set around elegant green cane tables and chairs. The tables had glass tops and pots with ferns and aspidistras were arranged here and there.

This was a great social asset to Tenby and why its loss is still mourned by those who knew and loved it.

It didn't matter what the weather was like. Here was an entertainment place to go as there were mostly afternoon matinées as well as the evening performances. Townspeople and visitors could enjoy meeting their friends for afternoon tea served by waitresses in black dresses with frilly caps and aprons.

All the matching china was attractive and in keeping with the décor. The cake stands had pedestals and the tea service were silver plated. On the cake stand would be an assortment of eight cakes: battenburg, fondants, cream sponge, fruit cake, eclairs, etc. Even if there was only one patron, this was their selection and they then paid for the amount eaten. Toasted teacakes, Welsh rarebit, scones, were all on the menu.

Afterwards they could go into the picture show. The usherettes or doormen, who wore bottle-green uniforms with little pillbox hats, took your ticket and gave you half back, and shining a long torch, showed you to your seat.

As children we wanted the front row, or the nearest to it. We didn't want to be behind a tall man or a lady with a big hat and miss something. We knew down there we were likely to find our friends.

Courting couples favoured the back row as this afforded a modicum of privacy. There were few places for couples to go to embrace, especially in the winter. So the cinema was very popular. There is no life without love, and few of us are fortunate enough to find our lifetime partner at our first attempt.

We often averted our eyes when passing the back row as couples would be locked in their own passions and seldom saw those on the screen.

We thought they must be mad as we had just watched with delight the movies of the day, so glamorous and exciting to small town children who knew nothing of the outside world.

Lovely blondes, Betty Grable and June Haver, danced and sang their way through the 'Dolly Sisters.' Just the material Wendy and I were looking for. We hoped the usherettes wouldn't notice if we stayed in for the next performance so that we could see it again to imitate in our games.

As you were allowed in at any stage of the performance the cinema wasn't always empty at the end. Some would be staying to see what they had missed. In order to accuse you of overstaying your welcome the usherette would have to remember what time you came in. Often the cinema was so full there would be standing room only and people would be packed in the aisles and along the back. The usherettes had their work cut out, as when one or two persons left, they would select the first people in the queue and show them to the vacant seats. This often involved a lot of people in the row standing up to let them pass. Some with babies who started to cry. Some with paper bags of windfall apples that rolled about the floor. Whilst all this went on those behind could no longer see and showed their objections quite loudly, especially as it was dark and no one knew who had shouted.

The performance at the cinema was double sided, but great fun. We revelled in it all, enjoying every moment. Sometimes the film broke down and there was an uproar of shouting, jeering and foot stamping until the hapless projector man could repair it.

We were so lucky in this respect as the film industry in this country and in Hollywood was at its peak.

Every week in Tenby there were at least four main feature films to choose from. There would be a fifteen-minute Pathé newsreel and then a 'short' film to make up the performance. Oh! The joy when it was one of our favourites: Mother Reilly, George Formby, Laurel and Hardy, or Robin Hood with Errol Flynn. He was one of my imaginary boyfriends, as was Burt Lancaster. I don't think I ever stopped loving him and could sob today at the sad loss of such a fine athletic man with so much charm. He had been a circus performer and did all his own stunts in his wonderful swashbuckling films. We were totally transported. How cruel is fate that this fine man should endure strokes in his later years and be in a wheelchair. How cruel for anyone.

On the dramatic side we had James Mason, Margaret Lockwood, Eric Portman, Clarke Gable, Vivian Leigh and so many more. All had flourishing careers in films and rose to fame as the industry tried to keep up with the insatiable demand.

Comedy was geared to suit the naïveté of the day, which is why we find it difficult to watch, to some extent, today when our tastes have become more sophisticated. Abbot and Costello and Laurel and Hardy are an example of this. But we roared with laughter at their antics. As we did at some of our parents' idols, Charlie Chaplin, Will Hay, Buster Keaton. These were mostly shown as the 'shorts' and must have given a welcome respite from the cares of the War to many adults as well as children.

Before the end of the performance you saw a 'trailer' advertising what was to come next. Our minds were already working on how we would get the necessary threepence each.

Nothing on Sundays in the form of entertainment. A deep hush settled on the town. Every public house was closed, every shop. The only sound was the milkman's horse clip-clopping on the streets as he delivered his milk. Or those of Mr Atwell's horses as he took them from their stables in

144 A TENBY LIFEBOAT FAMILY

Upper Frog Street to their grazing on the Marsh Road. Lively Arabs, they were far from quiet.

The liveliness of the town was of course due to the demand from the troops for entertainment. Everything was used to a maximum and because deep inside many people were insecure, homesick, lost and unhappy the precious moments of their leisure time were so important. Everything else was pushed to one side until it had to be faced again. 'Live for the Moment' was the motto of the day.

Another way we found of getting the picture-money was to collect and take back the pop bottles. Quite a lot of fizzy mineral water, which we called pop, was drank in those days as we didn't have the preservatives necessary to keep fruit juices that we have today, and in Tenby we even boasted our own pop works [on the Marsh Road, on the bend just past Newell Hill - the proprietor 'Mrs Thomas the Pop' was killed in 1941 when a German plane jettisoned its bombs over Tenby].

Everything is a game to little children and finding pop bottles was like hide-and-seek. We didn't have many at home, as money was needed for more basic food, so we had to seek them elsewhere in appropriate places, as people not concerned with the 'penny on the bottle' deposit would carelessly throw them on to the beach or in the long grass.

Delighted with every find, we took them home to wash them in mum's old washing bath in the garden. Once clean we sorted them into their dealers' names as the shopkeeper would only take back the brand that they sold.

We then had to find an old carrier bag to put them in. We didn't have plastic in those days. The brown paper carrier bags had string handles glued into the rim of the bag and were designed for one-off use. They cost pennies to buy so had to be kept and reused by us - and as it often rains in Tenby were in trouble when we either lost a handle or the paper disintegrated as we walked along and dropped the precious shopping on the road, or once, our pop bottles which went rolling at great speed down the Maudlins with us in pursuit, groping around in the kerbs, rescuing them to ensure we still had enough money to go to the pictures.

We took them to Fanny Davies on the Green or Mrs Lloyd's or the Evergreen Inn where we had to go to the back door, knock and wait for the man to come out.

I'm sure although we didn't realise it we must have been a nuisance at times, but we were never made to feel it. This poverty did no harm and it taught us to work hard for what we wanted and appreciate to the full the wonders of our childhood that we did enjoy.

Was it 'Tarzan' at the Royal Playhouse this week or the 'Man in Grey' at Shanly's South Beach Pavilion? Sometimes we weren't allowed in without an adult because of the film rating. We had to await a friendly adult who would take us in as their own and hoped no doubt to shake us off, so to speak, once inside. We didn't expect anything else. What we did to go to the pictures was unbelievable.

We once devised our own 'Pidgin English.' This entailed taking the first letter from a word and adding it to the end. This way we could speak to each other without our mother knowing what we were saying, or so we thought, until all of a sudden mother said: "No, you may not have the picture money!"

The cinema was a great money spinning industry at this time, employing thousands of talented people behind the scenes, as well as the noted stars.

It seems unbelievable that it fell to ruin, especially as even now, sixty years hence, we are still watching the same films.

I feel we were very privileged to have been able to enjoy all these features of our era.

The only sad part is the thought that it was Wartime, and for many there was a lot of personal sadness. A sense of loss and anxiety. After such a traumatic time, would life ever be the same again?

Enterprising as the needy have to be, we also were baby-sitting. I was too young for this but went as company for my older sisters, who really enjoyed looking after real live dolls.

We kept going in to peep at them sleeping so beautifully in their cots and beds, and hoped they would wake up soon so that we could change the thick towel nappy, intricately fastened in a three-corner shape with a big nappy pin at the front. We knew we had to put one hand under the folds before we inserted the pin so as not to harm the baby's tummy, and as the baby did not usually enjoy this procedure and often kicked, wriggled and cried, it was not easily achieved, so I had to hold it safe whilst my sister did the trick.

Once dry and upright the baby was usually delighted with the company of these funny little kids who had come to play with it. We took it in turns to give it milk in its bottle and we sang it every little nursery song we knew, and it didn't seem to mind a bit that we were out of tune, until it couldn't stay awake any longer, and we reluctantly laid it back in its cot.

For baby-sitting we were paid a shilling which we shared. Sometimes we were there until after midnight and it was a strange feeling, running home down the road in the dark, to creep indoors and up the stairs, trying not to make a noise, or we would have got shouted at. Our parents knew where we had been, but we never knew if they realised we were safely back. It was just taken for granted. Sometimes the lady's husband would see us down the road.

A lot of Officers' wives and young families followed their husbands around during the war. They rented any vacant houses in the town. Near us it was the Upper Maudlins, the Serpentine and Narberth Road. Our reliability was passed between them by word of mouth. We were asked to their children's parties and my elder sisters learned a lot from this experience as it was an essential training for their own motherhood days that were to come.

SAINT MARGARET'S FAIR

Quite a different entertainment from the cinema, but of equal delight to us was Saint Margaret's Fair, an annual event in Tenby.

It took place then on the South Parade against the old town wall. It took over the whole area down to the Five Arches.

I'm not sure how they coped for access, seeing that the Fire Station and several shops were also there. Plus the 'parade' was the town's bus terminus at that time, so other arrangements must have been made for them.

However Saint Margaret's Fair has a long historical lineage of coming to Tenby and a lot was waived in its favour.

Its stalls and booths were scattered all around. The traders' ornate caravans, carts and wagons squeezed into every nook. Their painted wooden steps boasted shining metal water carriers and curly-headed brown-skinned children.

First along the wall at the rear of the De Valence were the swinging-boats. Tame by today's standards, but quite an experience to us as we sat, one or two at each end of the swinging-boat, paid our penny and took it in turns to pull the rope which enabled us to swing higher and higher. We felt we might shoot over the town wall or even Saint John's Church tower opposite.

The roll-a-penny and hoop-la gave us a game and a chance to win a prize. One popular trophy of the day was an Alsatian dog ornament made from some kind of chalk compound, moulded and painted. Quite a few houses in our road had them as prized possessions. Reminders of a lucky win the previous year. I tried in vain to win one for my mother, but in retrospect I feel she would have hated it, as she had a yen of the finer things along those lines: figurines, Japanese china and cut glass. These she managed to acquire to some extent despite being poor as she was sometimes given such as this as a gift for bringing neighbours' babies into the world.

The coconut shy was not for me as I was too small to be effective. But the boys loved it as a challenge, as they did the shotguns that shot tiny feathered darts at cards on a stand and the stallholder checked their score and gave a prize accordingly.

As we would only have a few pennies to start with it didn't take long to spend. What took a long time was deciding which of these delights you should spend your money on. One day I was on my way home and had chosen to walk down the Norton so that I could see the sea whilst in town. I met an elderly neighbour, an old gentleman with a crooked spine which made him walk leaning backwards, not forward. Still he walked around town every day with the aid of a stick and he lived in Broadwell Hayes. He was very tall with white hair, very fair skin and bushy white eyebrows with deep-set blue eyes. I wish I could remember his name. He stopped to speak to me coming up the Norton and asked if I had been to the Fair. I said "Yes, Sir" and he said "And have you spent all your money?" And I said "Yes, thank you Sir." Then he took from his pocket a sixpence and he said, "Well now you go back and have a turn on everything for me."

I held the sixpence tight in my little warm hand. It was like the Crown Jewels to me. As I retrod my path, what should I buy? A toffee apple for a penny or hot chestnuts? I still can't make up my mind in a sweet shop! And what ride should I have? A go on the merry-go-round? We had never heard of the word 'carousel.'

A few years later, Saint Margaret's Fair included part of its venue at the Salterns on the Marsh Road as the rides had become larger and more sophisticated by this time. This space, where the caravan park now is, gave them more room for dodgems, merry-go-rounds, the waltzer and the ghost train. We had never seen these things before and couldn't wait to have a go. There were lots of little machines that for a penny gave you a printed card with your fortune on it, or a flickering picture view of some cheeky shots of 'What the Butler Saw' - Victorian ladies in various states of lacy undress spied through the keyhole. We thought they were hilarious.

During the time the Fair was in town we made the most of it, and went everyday, any money to spend or not. Just to be there amongst the strange atmosphere and look at the fairground people who had a certain brown tough appearance. Gypsy stock, hard-working, dedicated to their way of life. Their little children initiated into it from birth were on the stall with them, helping and learning. Always well behaved.

The barrel-organ music, which was so much a part of the scene, was unlike any we heard elsewhere. It seems to create a joyful atmosphere, and walking around you felt a light-hearted pleasure in being there, lost in another world for a short space of time. We had to be home by nine o'clock. Sometimes it was becoming dark as we walked home across the Green and up the Maudlins, chattering about what we had enjoyed the most. As we came to our friend's house we called: " 'night, call for you in the morning."

THE CIRCUS COMES TO TOWN

The other highlight of the year was the circus and joy of joy, where was it held? At the top of our road.

A week or two before its arrival, posters had been stuck on the various billboards around the town. The largest one of these was, and still is, on Greenhill Road, opposite the little plantation and close to the railway viaduct. We children loved this. It was our newspaper so to speak, telling us in big letters and colour pictures the events of the day. Often depicted in cartoon style. A lot of artistic work went into advertisements as photography was not as widely used as it is today. We learned to spell a lot of long words from it as we practised when we went back and forth to school.

They also posted the circus notices on the telegraph poles, and as they were too high for us to have a really close look, we took it in turns to jump on each other's backs to get a better look at what was coming, each asking the other were there monkeys? Were there lions? At no other time did we see these wild animals, except in the Tarzan films at the cinema, which were staunch favourites with all of us children and of many adults.

The field where the circus was held was the one where Tenby Infants School [opened in 1953] now stands in Heywood Lane - opposite the junction with Serpentine Road.

Circuses were a lot less sophisticated than they are today. This was the world famous Chipperfield Family Circus or Robert Brothers which even manages to get down to our small town. A big circus family, they no doubt had several small troupes touring the country and interchanged the acts and animals.

Agog with anticipation we could never be entirely sure of the direction from which it would arrive and we wanted to be as far up the road or down as possible to join in the procession.

If its previous venue was Saundersfoot then it would just come down the Narberth Road and go across the Serpentine. If it had just come from Pembroke, it would come across the Green and up our road which was a bit less steep than Heywood Lane.

The circus took advantage of their trek to the venue and showed their *artistés* and animals to advantage, therefore ensuring a full house. Pretty little ponies and horses were led along, the elephants walked in line holding each other's tails. The clowns gave out leaflets to all assembled on the pavement to watch them pass.

On one memorable occasion, as the circus trundled up the Maudlins, one of the two elephants decided to do a detour up

THE CIRCUS COMES TO TOWN

our drive. As dad always left one side of the gate open and against the wall for a quick exit to the Lifeboat, the elephant took advantage of this nice wide space with the aroma of apples and vegetables at the end of it and up he went. We were dancing up and down with excitement. Could we keep him? Our own elephant in our garden! Mother took a photo from the living room window. He was on the rockery gently snipping green apples from her one and only apple tree. I wish I still had the photograph.

He was ours for such a short time as one of the trainers came with a long pole and nudged him away before he did too much damage, and back up the road.

Still we were given two free tickets for the trouble! No trouble at all. We were delighted. And we could still see him at the performance, or free up the field where the circus animals were hobbled and just allowed to graze.

We decided to spend as much time as possible up at the circus field as the whole atmosphere was exciting and entertaining.

What hard-working people they were. As with the gypsies and fairground people, the same group did everything. First the Big Top had got to be unloaded and erected, and this was a mammoth task with no equipment other than pulleys.

The high centre-pole was positioned. Men held ropes which ran from the top of the pole until it was secured and then the same men heaved and heaved on the tent ropes until the Big Top was raised. Then came the knocking in of tent pegs all around.

Others carried in drums and planks to make up the seating and curved red and white blocks which formed the Circus Ring, the inner of which was filled with thick sawdust. As the lower part of the Big Top had loose air flaps all around the bottom, little imps like us could keep having a peep to see how things were progressing.

The outer edges of the field were lined with the gypsy-type wagons that the circus people lived in and used as their dressing rooms. We were very attracted to them and lingered around and stared as children stare.

Often the top part of a caravan's door would be open and we could see the pretty china and curtains inside. As they seemed more child size than a house we thought them much nicer and would love to have played in one of them.

The booking office was a small tent, like a Punch and Judy Show tent, and as soon as this was open at ten o'clock in the morning, so our townsfolk arrived to buy tickets. This ensured a perch on a plank and a quicker entry than otherwise queuing for tickets at the time of the performance.

We were used to queuing in those days. We queued for everything, usually quite good-naturedly, but not always. If someone pushed in and jumped the queue so to speak, those patiently waiting let them know about it, quite rightly.

The queue for the circus tickets was like a wild animal in itself. It stretched across the field like an unruly crocodile. Those children, held by their parents' hands to wait, wriggled and cried as they wanted to be off, having a peep at the animals in cages and the little ponies and llamas.

We didn't have this problem. Oh the freedom. It made up for any neglect and we had to remember that.

The first performance was at two o'clock. We had to be home for dinner at twelve am, so as soon as that was eaten, without any noticeable gobbling, we hoped, we would ask to be excused to get down from the table and go back out to play. We never left the table without asking if we may, and we never helped ourselves to food without asking "May we have ... ?" and "Thank you."

By one o'clock the queue for tickets for the matinée was forming and another one for ticket-holders lining up to go in and get a ringside seat. At any time the notice to say 'House Full' may be erected and the disappointed children would have to wait for the next performance at seven pm.

I don't suppose the circus people had more than a hour's break between the two shows, and when finished and it was

THE CIRCUS COMES TO TOWN

getting dark they still had to see to the animals. Rub down the sweating horses and bed them for the night. Acrobats, they wouldn't have eaten between performances, so they would have a late meal before bed.

Many would have been born to this and knew no other way of life. The others, *artistés*, often came from other countries where they had perfected their performance and would move from one circus to another from time to time as novelty was the catchword.

Alongside all the traditional things that the audience expected to see, the clowns, the bareback horse-riding, the pretty ladies standing on horses' backs doing ballet steps, the little dogs jumping through hoops and pulling little carts with puppies in, the ringmaster in his top hat and tails introducing the acts ... and then the *artistés*! Trapeze and high wire acrobats swinging up in the ceiling of the Big Top.

Wendy, Beryl and I were picking up tips all the time. This was material to enrich our games. Beryl was the swinger, regardless of self-imposed injury. She had to date put both arms out of their sockets, broken one, and split her lip whilst swinging. Also nearly hung herself on a couple of occasions. But went on undeterred and highly respected in the gang for her daring and bravery.

Wendy and I on the other hand were ambitious but timid which produced a strange effect at times. We were enraptured with the pretty lady in star spangled tights on the tightrope, and we knew we were quite good at balancing on the top of walls, so we thought we'd have a go at this. But where would we find a tightrope?

One of our friends who lived down our road at the top of the Paddock in the Jubilee, was honoured by our company at times. She lived in a quiet spot and her father was a policeman, an only child she wasn't allowed to run around like us.

Part of her garden was an orchard of large apple trees. Her mother hung the washing-line from tree to tree. Just the very place. We tightened up the washing-line as well as we could. Thin rope used to be used in those days and then we climbed a tree, one either end of the line. We hoped to meet in the middle for moral support.

We held on to the tree branches to start with to get the feel of the rope before we dare let go. We knew we would have to hold out our arms in order to balance. So with great daring we took off. One or two little wobbles and over we went, down into a lovely bed of stinging nettles growing underneath. I'm not sure if we were laughing or crying. Apart from being covered all over with white stinging bumps we were unharmed. Our friend's mother came to the rescue, and as there was rather a lot of affected body areas to dab she put us naked in the bath and splashed malt vinegar on us. Not quite as glamorous as star spangled tights.

At the circus, when the elephants came into the ring, the house was in an uproar as the huge beasts bellowed and sat up and begged for titbits. They gently stepped over the pretty lady laid on the ground and then picked her up with their trunk and carried her. She even put her head in their mouths as they carried her around. We thought they were the most clever animals in the world and the most endearing.

Although we still wanted to watch we were a bit afraid of the lions. The lion-tamer held a wooden chair in one hand and a whip in the other as a defence against the snarling beasts. We had no wish to be a lion-tamer. Apart from the lions, the cage would have been unbearable.

All too soon their week was over. They rested on Sundays and then early on Monday morning they were up and away.

We hoped they were pleased they came to Tenby and we looked forward to seeing them again. Next year.

GYPSIES OF KILGETTY COMMON

I was offered a treat on one occasion, after mum had left home. A coach trip had been arranged for the children in the town. A rarity in those times.

With living in Tenby, we seldom went on the bus. The cost was sixpence and I didn't know if I would be allowed. I explained to my sister Barbara that Wendy was going and it was a Mystery Tour, and I loved mysteries. Barbara decided that as long as I went without at another time I should be allowed to go. The sixpence was found from the one-shilling and nine-pence housekeeping money dad left on the mantel-piece each morning before going to Tenby Lifeboat Station. The nine-pence was always in pennies which were intended for the gas, which we hoped wouldn't go out before she had cooked his dinner.

He was very much a 'meat and two veg' man and expected a pudding or 'afters' as we children called it. Roly-poly and custard or apple pie.

Barbara could always be relied on to have a feeling for the occasion and she worked hard in getting me ready. Some suitable clothes were found. A cotton dress and cardigan. I had a good wash in the bathroom and then came the painful procedure. My hair. My long thick plaits were unbraided and found to be full of tangles. Barbara got frustrated with it, so Beryl was called to aid. Beryl had a strong arm due to muscle build up when she swung from branch to branch of the trees, aping Tarzan at the cinema. That was a favourite playtime. She was Tarzan, I was Jane. I hung on to the bedposts bravely whilst she tugged the wire brush through my tangles, and at one point 'ouched' too much, so got a smack on the back of the head with a hairbrush. As I was nearly always on the verge of tears, being the emotional one in the family, my sobbing was ignored. If you want to go you have to get ready.

156 A TENBY LIFEBOAT FAMILY

The coach stopped in the Maudlins and Wendy and I got on. It was already quite full of children from up the town, so we pushed our way to the back. We were quite excited about a Mystery Tour, having no idea what it meant. How the driver kept his cool with all us chattering children I don't know, but we didn't jump up and down as we knew this wasn't allowed. We just wriggled.

Up the Narberth Road. We were used to walking to Waterwynch but not much further. New Hedges, where we knew some of our classmates came from, and Saundersfoot which, would you believe, we had never seen in our ten young years. On then to Kilgetty, and there on the Common was a wondrous sight indeed. A gypsy encampment crammed with colourful wagons, tents, fires, horses, children running at play, dogs barking behind them. A different race from us, living on the open Common, its middle crossed by the road, with little to shelter them from the elements, or give them privacy.

The coach turned off the road to Narberth at Templeton and the journey home was past Carew Castle. It was a part of the world I had never seen and had quite an effect on me, as mentally I decided to find out more and more about these fascinating gypsies and the history of the beautiful castle.

I will tell you a little now about the Romany gypsies and the part they played in our lives in Tenby. On a personal note I feel they influenced my mother into leaving us with their fortune telling. In the thirties and forties, Pembrokeshire was the home of many gypsies. Some true Romanys, some not.

The true Romanys were descendants from the Egyptians. They were a proud race with a strict code of conduct.

Kilgetty Common was crowded with their colourful wagons called *vardos*. These were highly sought after as they were custom-made by skilled wheelwrights across the country. Made from ash, the carriage part was solidly built on a strong frame. The wheels were also made from wood

GYPSIES OF KILGETTY COMMON

and faced with steel bands. At the front of the *vardo* they had an ornate wooden door and bow-windows either side. Apart from the front and back framework, the top was made of arch shaped ash wands and green canvas was stretched tightly across it and secured down. The inside of the roof was lined for comfort sometimes with brightly coloured fabric.

The layout inside was designed to suit the gypsy and beds had to be made with a dual purpose and used as seats in the daytime. Every inch of space was utilised from the chassis to the roof.

Obviously this wagon was their most prized possession, but such is their creed that on the death of the owner the *vardo* would be burned to the ground.

Is there a moral in there somewhere? That all must have their own goal in life to work for?

Although regarded by many as heathens, they did in fact have their *chavvies* christened in Church and interred their dead in Church graveyards along the way. Some of the christenings could be taken tongue-in-cheek as the same *chavvie* was often baptised several times as they passed from parish to parish and often vicars concerned about their souls would offer them a shilling in return for having the baby christened. This they gladly took and smiled at the vicar's ignorance.

When planning to move on, a council was held as to the route and destination. Often several families travelled together. A well-trod path around the countryside, they knew all the bounties to be found en route.

Their flat Dray Carts colourfully painted were used to transport all the miscellaneous items. Piled high with basketwork creels containing quacking ducks, clucking hens and geese.

The goats and dogs were tethered behind and the smaller *chavvies* dumped on top in any little nook. The gypsy women and young girls, *chies*, walked at the rear. The men and the young men, *rais*, walked at the horse's head and often led spare horses. These horses were of Arab descent, strong, lively and colourful piebalds.

What a sight this gypsy train was to see as it trundled along the road. Horses' thick manes and tails blowing in the breeze. Curly-headed children, barefooted in ragged clothes. Women draped in yards of different coloured skirts and shawls. Amongst the tribe they would have their own farrier and vet for the animals. Their own healer for themselves. A self-contained race.

Proud and independent, their only need from us *gorgios*, as we were known to them, was money. We were their trading ground. They did not actually beg, they acquired by hawking.

The women and *chies*, together with any *chavvies*, called at the back door of a house. The women had a large flat basket on her arm which held a variety of nicely arranged items for sale. These included handmade clothes-pegs, made by two sticks being whittled to shape and bound together with a band of tin. They were the best clothes-pegs ever. Decorative wooden flowers which looked like chrysanthemums were skilfully whittled and dyed in bright shades. The heads were fastened on to thin sticks and often fell off. Sometimes the flowers arranged for the 'kind lady' were made of coloured paper, and sometimes gathered from the hedgerows; violets, primroses, heather, clover. The buyer was persuaded that the purchase would bring luck. At times the basket would be full of yards of lace and elastic at threepence or sixpence a yard. Underwear had to be repaired in those days in order to last and knickers' elastic in our house, with so many girls, was an essential item.

At the same time as they tried to sell they asked, "Had the kind lady any clean rags?" For their *chavvies*, any items of clothing were acceptable to them and they would sometimes give coppers in return. Their horse and cart would be creeping down the road as they called from house to house.

On one occasion we were cheated, so to speak, as my mother had given the gypsy a lot of rags - and they must have been rags if we had finished with them! She told my mother she would pay a shilling, so Beryl and I were sent with the gypsy to the cart to collect it. She climbed up on the cart, turned it in the road, whipped the horse "Gee up!" and off she trotted. Beryl and I instinctively followed in pursuit of mother's shilling. She shot off round the Serpentine Road with us still running, but she lost us going down the Heywood Lane as by now we were breathless and had a pain in the side - 'stitch' as we called it. We didn't know whether to laugh or cry as we sat down on the kerb and we still had to go home and tell mother.

My mother was herself a bit psychic and she often asked the gypsies in to sit around the fire, drink leafy tea, and read the tea-leaves. I was fascinated by their conversation and often hid behind the sofa, so that my mother forgot I was there.

One Amazon-type gypsy who had gold sovereigns plaited into her dark hair had a strange effect on the gas cooker, which was just inside the back door. Whenever she entered the kitchen the gas under the kettle went out. This happened every time. She was always referred to by us as the gypsy who made the gas go 'pop!'

Their fortune telling, as with all their way of life followed a strict procedure. The tea was brewed in a big brown pot and was stirred three times. The adults concerned drank their tea to the dregs. The cup was then inverted over the saucer to drain any remaining liquid. The cup was then turned three times by the client in a clockwise direction. The gypsy then took the cup and read the fortune from the shapes that the tea-leaves had formed inside the cup.

There was a horseshoe, which was lucky. The kind lady was coming into money. There was a letter for the lady. It was large. Maybe a parcel. There was a tall dark stranger in the cup. Childbirth, death, hope and omens.

I do know from personal experience that certain gypsies have psychic power. I believe they use the tea-leaves, palms, crystal balls, etc as an acceptable medium for this.

My own fortune was told by one in adult life. No medium was used, neither had I asked for a telling. She just came into my shop, looked across at me and said: "I won't see you again. You are going back to Wales to live, you will live on the Milford Haven and have a business like this and you will be lucky." All of which came true.

Some several years after this I was in my shop in Milford Haven. Another gypsy came into my shop. She asked me to weigh a banana for her little girl. I took the banana and gave it to the child. I did not want payment remembering what it was like to be poor from my childhood. I touched the child on her curly-head as her fairness reminded me of Beryl.

The gypsy immediately started to tell my fortune and everything she said was true.

I myself have some ability to read the Tarot Cards. I don't know if it is inherited from mother or if I have just found it easy to learn because I was fascinated by gypsies.

Even more than us, they lived close to the ground and enjoyed its wonders to the full. The singing of the birds, the flowers that grew in the fields, hedgerows and marshes. The herbs that they gathered for cooking and medicine. They were so much wiser than us.

Their encampment was called a *tan*. A good encampment was a *kushti tan*. They had their regular *tans* and on leaving it to travel on would leave secret messages for the next Romanys by arranging sticks and bunches of grass in certain patterns.

On a long trek, they just briefly stopped overnight. Had their main meal of the day, usually fatty bacon fried with lard. When travelling the women did not have the opportunity to do the daily bake, so bread had to be bought for supper en route and the money earned by hawking along the way. In the morning they rose early. Once again their meal was bread and what was left of the bacon. They revived the dying embers of the fire and brewed hot strong sweet tea. They would not eat again until evening and had far to go.

The men were fed first. They attended to the animals and all was made fast for the journey. The used crockery was carefully wrapped in newspaper, the sooty pots and pans stowed inside the pan-box which was underneath the *vardo*. Bender-tents, *shako*, were dismantled and stacked on the open carts. Steps that led up to the *vardos* were unhooked and put in their place beneath the food cupboard called a *cratch*.

On their journey the gypsy only rides on cart or wagon on flat ground. At any hill they jump down and walk out of consideration for their horses whose load is already heavy, and who are as essential to them as food.

Sometimes going up hill the horses would be used two together to take the strain. The method used was to take the horse from one wagon and place in traces in front of another. When the top of the hill was reached both horses would be taken back down the hill to fetch the next wagon. This practice was called doubling-up. A wooden wedge was used at intervals on the hill to hold the wheels and give the horses a break.

If a lot of *vardos* were travelling together on an overnight *tan* they would be arranged in a circle for maximum protection and one or two would be placed across the field entrance as a deterrent to the horses straying.

The women rose first in the morning seeking willow and green ash for fire tinder. Filling the water *jacks* from the nearest stream, they hung the big black kettle on the *chittie*, the iron hook on a frame over the fire, to boil the water for their strong tea.

This they felt gave stamina and energy to sustain them through the day. They ate swiftly with their brown fingers and, strangely, drank from fine bone china cups.

The winter was a difficult time for them as it is for all who live in the great outdoors. It carried away the old and sick and they buried them in sacred ground as they passed a village churchyard.

Spring brought new life and the prospect of work on the farm. At this time the amount of machinery and equipment a farmer owned was very small, amounting to a humble plough which was pulled between two work horses, or sometimes if he was exceptionally lucky one of the early tractors.

The farm land had to be cultivated by hand, and most of our Pembrokeshire farms employed three or four farm labourers on a permanent basis, but when it came to intensive times, casual labour in the form of gypsies came into play. Weeding, sowing, potato planting and picking, carrots, peas, beans and swede. Much was secreted to go back to the *tan* for stock and tasty meals. Hay, corn and rye, wheat and silage. The harvest of the land.

The gypsy men and *rais* took pride in their physical strength and worked at muscle building when using their sledge hammers around the *tan*. With a fit body your hard labour was achieved more easily and with their meagre diet they were lean of limb.

From toddler age the *chavvies* and *rais* aped their fathers in following the male behaviour. Each of the tribe dependent on the other for survival, each had to fulfil a role.

Their work was hard. Their hours long. The care of their horses was paramount and had to be done at the end of the day, however tired they were. Always on the move, the work of setting up or dismantling the *tan* was repetitive and arduous. The travelling itself brought change of scene and lightness of spirit. Any problems with farmers and villagers were left behind, shaken off as on they went to pastures new.

The *chavvies* were acutely intelligent as senses hone in to help us with our environment. They had to live with their wits and so became adept. They were unschooled as they would seldom be in one place long enough. Their parents were illiterate as well, so they couldn't teach them these *gorgios* skills. But in their own life they had little use for them and ignorant or lazy they certainly were not.

Some of the Romany women were very house-proud of their *vardos*. They gleamed with care and detail. A well kept one was a sight to see.

The black pot-belly stove with brass fiddle-rail, which was their mainstay apart from the communal fire, gleamed with much polishing with Zebra, a black liquid cleaner we used at home. It had a special spirit smell, it was a sort of mixture of charcoal and spirit which was nice. Like furniture polish, it smelled of care.

Colour is very important to a gypsy and the brighter the better. Pattern is intermixed with pattern. Within the small space of the *vardo* all they owned was on display. There was a brilliant array of colour and luxurious fabrics. Curtains, pelmets with fringes, bed covers, cushions, velvet, satin, silk and damask. All was sought after and added. They valued fine china and coveted that in bold red and blue and gold. This adorned the many shelves, fitted with guard-rails, and underneath cups and jugs hung from the many hooks. All were wrapped and stacked away before a move. Teapots, crystal, silver, brass, old brass lamps and pictures with tasselled frames. Nothing was too fancy.

The self-made rugs were bright and striped, hand-woven and colour dyed from the lichen and flower petal dyes. At the entrance to the *vardo* the ornate door and bow-windows were swathed with lace curtains tied back by coloured ribbons.

When a person has very little, what they do have becomes very precious to them as I know. A great deal more than it ever does when you have plenty. I have seen both sides of the coin so to speak. As have many others of my generation, and when conversing on this subject we invariably say we were happier then. Isn't life strange?

Speaking personally, I feel it was the wonderful feeling of freedom which enabled us to go, whenever and wherever we chose without fear from our society. Unfortunately we can't say that today and we are all robbed as a consequence. No material possession can make up for that, however costly.

The young female *chie* slept within the *vardo* with their parents. The male *rais* slept outside in the *shako* bender-tents. Thus was the female morality guarded. They prized virginity and as with the upper classes of the *gorgio* society they exchanged their girls for money. The more attractive the bride the higher the agreed bride-purse. They seldom married out of their race and creed and council would be held to vet a proposed suitor.

Until the marriage the couple would always have a chaperone, usually the *chie's* grandmother.

To form an official council to discuss these matters a large pole was hammered into the ground. This was the centre-piece of the circle that they formed around it to discuss the issue and it was called a *peeled-stick*. No official council was held without it and they had to wait until family members arrived from various parts of the country before it could begin. If a good bride-purse was achieved, much jollity commenced. Men slapped each other on the back and shook hands all round.

In return for the bride-purse the father of the bride gave, if he could afford it, a new *vardo* to the betrothed couple. If this was not possible the couple started their married life in a *shako* bender-tent. Made from arch-shaped hazel wands, eight parallel holes were dug, four either side. A wand was inserted in one hole and bent over and inserted in the hole facing it. When the arch was completed a blanket was thrown over and then a green waterproof canvas. These were firmly secured. The floor inside was covered with a thick layer of clean straw, and the future home was ready.

The actual marriage ceremony was very simple. The betrothed couple stood facing each other at the *peeled-stick*.

The council and the rest of the tribe sat around the circle. The bride's father gave the couple one piece of dry bread offered on a plate. The bride and groom each broke off a small piece and ate it.

Now they were solemnly married. Divorce was nearly as easy, as in their law they may leave their partner if they wish to after the marriage has lasted seven years.

Traditional merriment took place after the betrothal. Men and *rais* jumped over the camp-fire whilst the onlookers clapped and encouraged their daring and laughed as some were seen to hold their singed bottoms rather painfully.

Broomsticks were then held out like hurdles and they leaped over them.

Out came the fiddles and the musicians amongst them started the dancing, joined by those with the humble tin whistle and reed flute. The *chies* with their be-ribboned tambourines all danced in celebration.

ROYAL INFLUENCES

Through each generation we are influenced by the behaviour of the society in which we live. As children we are also influenced by the effect that the previous era had on our parents.

The Royal Family of the day set the code to follow as our parents were a similar age to David the Duke of Windsor, who was to abdicate and Bertie, Duke of York, who was to become King George VI and father to our present Queen.

When I researched the narration I now follow with, it was brought home to me the very strict, even cruel treatment of children in my parents' time, and because of this I can understand to some extent their attitude to us as it was the order of the day so to speak and not uncommon.

It is only in these later years that these things have come to light. Through the openness of the media.

Before their parents were crowned King and Queen, but in preparation for it, they lived in York Cottage on the Sandringham Estate in Norfolk. David was born in 1894 and Bertie in 1895. Their parents were to have four more children, although these four never had to suffer quite as much as David and Bertie.

York Cottage was not a big house by Royal standards and the children's nursery quarters were small and cramped. Their first nanny, Mrs Green was a neurotic sadist. She showed a perverted affection for David and ignored Bertie completely. Even neglecting to feed him.

Both little boys developed complexes and Bertie had nerve and stomach problems and was unable to speak without stammering. Her sly cruelty towards them went undetected for three years, until she had a nervous breakdown.

The last thing they needed was a cruel nanny as their parents were remote and even cruel.

Their father was a repressive figure. A dark influence in their lives. They longed to be alone with their mother, but the time they spent with her was restricted to short, formal visits.

Occasionally they were allowed to join her in her boudoir, in the hour before dinner where Mary gave them her attention for a short time. Attention to duty was never forgotten, even in these precious moments. Sometimes she read the Classics to them but they were not enjoyable pastimes for small boys. Nevertheless they treasured them.

On one occasion Mary presented David with a rag doll she had made for him of a chimney-sweep. This became his most prized possession. A mascot to go with him on all his travels, even when adult.

Those who knew Mary through her life said that she was a cold, stiff person. Unmaternal. In fact she did want to be loved by her children but not at the expense of irritating her husband who actively disliked small boys and wanted as little as possible to do with them. Neither parent had any understanding of a child's mind.

Like all of us they carried with them the effect of their own past, and strange mixture that they were, they had little to offer their children. The indoctrination was that a child should be made to suffer for its own good and this belief was carried on for many years. Neither were children allowed an opinion, and at all times were supposed to be seen but not heard.

The little Princes lived in terror of their father's retribution. However small the wrong doing they were summoned to the library to be admonished and reproved. The older the boys became the worse their father's wrath as he feared he was losing dominance.

He often resorted to uncontrolled rage. Their mother would never intervene on their behalf. She lacked character and her background was such that she had been made to feel inferior by her husband's family who said that she came from the poverty-stricken scandal-haunted Tecks, who were in the lower divisions of European Royalty.

By marrying George she had redeemed her background and satisfied yearning for position. As mother of a future King, and Emperor, as one of her sons was to become, she determined to be 'queenlier' than any of them, and this rancour was her guiding light, at the expense of her children.

Their father mistrusted education saying that the naval training they would receive when old enough would teach them all they needed to know. This denied them the opportunity of making friends and playing with other children.

So they were kept at home with a tutor, Henry Hansell. His teaching was hopelessly inadequate, and neither of the boys advanced. Bertie already had an inferiority complex and this was made worse by his inability to grasp arithmetic and increased his stammer which was to beset him for the rest of his life.

Mrs Green, his first nanny, had imprinted in his mind that compared with his brother David he was worthless. Every way he turned he was put down. He was a natural sportsman and like many talented people he was left-handed. This appalled his father who had him forced to use his right hand. This put him at a great disadvantage and his confidence got worse as did his stammer. The more he stammered the more his father bellowed at him as he struggled to speak. He was only eight or nine at the time. The misery and cruelty in their life was appalling.

Always looking for faults where he expected perfection his father noticed that Bertie was knock-kneed and ordered that this should corrected by wearing splints on his legs for several hours a day. He wanted his legs to be right so he persevered bravely. But hardest of all was keeping them on at night in bed. His sobbing touched the heart of his valet who would remove them. But then the valet would be subjected to George's wrath.

In the end the splints did their job, but the emotional scars stayed for life. One on occasion of confrontation between George V and the valet on the splint matter, George stood up, pulled his trousers tight to his Royal legs to reveal his own knock-knees and shouted at the valet: "If that boy's legs grow up to look like this it will be your fault!"

In 1907, when David was just thirteen he was sent to Naval College at Osborne on the Isle of Wight. Most of the fears and antagonisms which would ultimately bring about his abdication were already ingrained.

The first taste of naval life would have been daunting in those days to any boy coming from a loving home. For David it can only be imagined.

He had been brought up with little or no contact with other children. At Osborne he was suddenly surrounded by strange boys for twenty-four hours a day. The senior cadets chided his every move.

ROYAL INFLUENCES 169

On one occasion his head was pushed out of the window and the sash was pulled down over his neck. A reminder to him of the fate of his ancestor Charles I. Another occasion red ink was poured down the front of his shirt.

Ragging and bullying were rife in the colleges of the day. Some may have been prepared for it having gone to 'prep' schools. David was experiencing it for the first time and was complete demoralised.

He had no one to talk to about it as he would have only got reproof and admonishment from his father. He was expected to act as a naval officer at fourteen.

Some parents of the day thought they owned their children and made their lives a misery, forcing them to conform to their ideals.

Each human is an individual and sink or swim should have some element of choice in their destiny.

When Bertie arrived at Osborne, owing to the division between the grades, David was not able to do much to help him adjust.

Bertie stoically followed David's example, suffering in silence through the loneliness, homesickness and bullying. Although he eventually became more popular than his elder brother.

By the end of David's three-year term of training at Osborne, Bertie and David had become the sons of a King [George V] as their grandfather Edward VII died on May 6th 1910.

In a new ceremony, dreamed up by the Chancellor of the Exchequer, David Lloyd George, David went to be invested as Prince of Wales in Caernarfon Castle. By this time he was already established in the public eye as a fairy-tale Prince Charming.

As David took the social limelight, so Bertie slid further into the shadows. He loved and revered his brother, but his inferiority complex made him increasingly resentful that he should always be regarded as second-best.

But as the two brothers grew towards manhood they began to enjoy themselves as they were able to spend some time away from home.

David went to Oxford University and toured Germany to visit his relations.

Bertie travelled the world as a midshipman in the Navy, enjoying the social life that it afforded.

The 1914-18 War was declared and David became a dashing officer, idolised by the troops he visited on the front line. Stuck in mud trenches, fighting for their country and trying to stay alive, God knows they needed all the support that they could get.

Once again Bertie was outshone. He still had nervous stomach disorders, the cause of which dated back to nursery days. When depressed he felt that nothing in life was in his favour. He remained isolated, humiliated and in pain for four years whilst he watched the rest of his generation fight and die for their country.

Although David appeared more confident he did realise that it was for his position as Prince of Wales that he was being lauded and not for any personal achievement of his own.

They had never been given any praise and encouragement and so had little sense of achievement.

They still lived in fear of their parents, their father's constant carping and demoralising rebukes. Neither of them were allowed any close, outside friends.

But David was soon to have other things on his mind. He started to show an avid interest in the opposite sex. He was in his early twenties in Amiens, France, when he was guided by his equerries towards a brothel, where they plied him with drinks before his initiation. Once having tasted the 'wine of life' he could think of nothing else. One 'lady of the night,' Maggie, who he spent a lot of time with later attempted to blackmail him.

Like his grandfather Edward VII he had fallen in love with womankind. A passion which lasted the rest of his life. There were to be many flames and one long lasting affair before that passion would find its consummation and nemesis. In Wallace Simpson.

David became in January 1936 our King [Edward VIII] and his relationship with Wallace Simpson, an American who had previously twice married and divorced, was not permitted. David abdicated on 11th December 1936. He had no intention of spending the rest of his life without love. This was the fun-loving David's choice. The woman who rocked the world, and brought shame on the British Throne.

But love they must have had as, married in 1937, they lived in exile together for the rest of their lives. Cast out by our Royal Family the rejection was continued until their death.

On David's abdication Bertie was to become King [George VI]. He had no desire for this elevation, despite always being in his brother's shadow. But duty was inescapable, as it always had been, and this dear, stuttering man, who hadn't a mean bone in his body had now one of life's greatest assets: a wonderful wife. Elizabeth Bowes-Lyon, who could not have been more charming, loving, caring and beautiful.

Added to which she had compassion for her subjects and helped so many that were worse off.

She gave Bertie the confidence he sorely needed, and it was only when he made his official speeches over the radio about the War that we were aware of his stammer. With his wife beside him he could at last face anything.

SAD FAREWELL TO TENBY

However secure we feel with our way of life we all know it is a moving platform.

The first to leave home was the eldest Dora. She had met a tall good-looking American, Lee Galloway, while at home on one of her holidays in May 1942. He had fallen very much in love with her, but had to go on Active Service then back to the States with his unit.

He served in Northern France and Belgium, and was decorated with a Bronze Medal following the decisive Battle of the Bulge, after which we were destined to victory and Germany was doomed to defeat.

He had been stationed with an armoured infantry battalion under canvas up in the Preseli Mountains at Rosebush, and whilst training at the Castlemartin tank range had attended a dance at the De Valence where they met.

She hadn't decided on marriage, but he had. Once back home his parents wrote and asked Dora to come to California for a holiday. Following 'demob' Lee became a student at the Berkley campus of the University of California, from which he graduated in 1948, and married Dora in May of that year.

At the Birmingham firm Dora had worked for, a colleague had a daughter going to the USA also, and it was arranged for them to accompany one another on board ship. They sailed the Atlantic Ocean on the *Queen Mary* with Dora then travelling across America by rail to California.

Dora was obviously taken with this new lifestyle, as we were to receive beautiful photographs of her wedding shortly afterwards.

It was very much a love-match, and has been a happy marriage lasting so far over fifty odd years. They spent their Golden Wedding Anniversary at the Royal Gate House Hotel in Tenby. Lee progressed in his legal carer to the position of Judge in the United States' Tax Courts on retirement, and they have two lovely daughters, Tenby and Rai.

Joyce the second eldest, married next. She met her husband Jack Lunn at the De Valence in April 1945. He was stationed at Saint Bride's Hotel, Saundersfoot with the Royal Marine Commandos, having seen Active Service in Sicily and Italy, and during the D-Day Landings he landed on Sword Beach in Normandy.

SAD FAREWELL TO TENBY 173

They married later that year at Wakefield in Yorkshire, his home town. As an Ex-Service girl from the Wrens, Joyce was able to borrow a beautiful wedding outfit from the film studios. This was a privilege given to some, and welcome, as money and clothing coupons were in short supply. This also was a love-match and has lasted fifty odd years. They have continued to live in the North, and had three fine sons, one sadly died of cancer.

Peggy the third eldest, our pretty princess, married her dark handsome soldier at Saint Mary's Church. Beryl and I were bridesmaids. Nylon had just come into fashion, and T P Hughes had a display of the fabric in their window. Peggy chose a few yards of blue for Beryl's fairness, and pink for my dark colouring. She made the long dresses by hand, as we didn't own a machine. Puff sleeves, and pin tucks, she made tiny roses from the contrasting colours and stitched them on. Never allowed to be extravagant, our new shoes for the occasion had to be plain brown lace-ups so that they could be used for school afterwards. She borrowed her gown and veil from a friend. Her slim shapely figure looked beautiful in white satin, with sweetheart neck and diamond shaping in the bodice. Her husband wore his Sergeant's Army uniform. After the ceremony we all went to Squibbs' Studios in Warren Street for the photographs, which are still good to this day. Then home for a wedding tea joined by some of our neighbours. In those days when someone in the road was getting married, neighbours all stood outside their gates to wave to them as they drove by.

Although Bert Overthrow, had striking good looks, and appeared to worship her on the one hand, she met with a lot of unkindness on the other. Both loved children, and this frail little girl gave birth to eight, two of them twins which died at a six-month pregnancy. But she must have been meant to have twins as her last pregnancy was twin girls, and they have been such comfort to her. Her husband died of heart trouble in his forties and Peggy has never remarried.

She has had serious health problems, and come out of them her usual beautiful self.

Barbara, tall with dark curly hair and brown eyes, was a very pretty young lady. A kind and loving nature made her popular with friends, family and animals. She was fourteen when mother left home, and looked after Beryl, Alan and I. In fact we were cleaner and better cared for than previously. She was a nice cook, expected some help from us with the household tasks, but was always fair.

At this time I passed for Greenhill Grammar School and dad gave Barbara the money to buy my uniform. I can't remember the name of the shop in town but it was next to newsagent W H Smith in High Street, a top outfitters [Stephen Davies]. I couldn't believe my luck, having all these new things at once in navy and gold gymslips and white blouses. So fair was she that with a pound or two left over from buying the uniform, she took me to T P Hughes to buy a pretty little flowered dress.

For about a year she cared for us, and was upset when she was usurped from her position, by a lady who was to come to live with us, and change our lives for the worse. She and her husband Bert Jenkinson had met our father at Tenby Lifeboat Station as he was a marine construction worker, and renovations were being made to the Lifeboat Slip. He and Joan were looking for accommodation in Tenby during their stay, and dad offered them to live at our house rent-free if Joan would act as housekeeper in our mother's absence. I suppose that dad felt that Barbara would be relieved by this move, but it didn't work out like that. Barbara was upset and left home taking a living-in job, for an Army Captain's family in a big house near the Bowling Green.

Spiteful as this Joan Jenkinson was, we younger ones were forbidden to talk to Barbara if we saw her in town. The summer holidays were passing, and I didn't know Beryl was also upset by Joan Jenkinson, but one day in town for some messages Beryl and I met Barbara on the South Parade, just

SAD FAREWELL TO TENBY

by chance. She was so pleased to see us. We were soaked with the rain, and her employers were abroad in Canada, so she asked us back to the house for a hot drink and to dry our clothes. Barbara told Beryl that she had mother's address. When Beryl and I got home there was a pile of dirty dishes in the sink, waiting for us to wash, and as we were late and couldn't say why, we were punished and sent to bed without tea.

In the middle of the night I was awoken by my father, and taken into his bed, very unusual. There I was questioned as to what had happened that day. He told me Beryl had run away, and we might have to get the police. I was very shocked and frightened. Beryl had been sleeping beside me, and I hadn't known she had gone into the small bedroom out on to the porch roof and down the drainpipe.

Honesty was natural to us children, whatever the consequences. So I told my father that we had met Barbara and that Beryl had probably gone to her, as she was in the big house on her own. Dad let me go back to my bed, telling me that it would be alright, and later that day Barbara called at the house for Beryl's ration book. Which Joan Jenkinson threw at her. Barbara got in touch with mother, who was living by this time in a tied cottage on the Lancashire moors with Tom Greenwood.

Barbara had been writing to a boyfriend Al Harmen, who was a paratrooper stationed near Tenby. He was very much in love with her, and still is. She left Tenby to marry him, and lived in his home town of Watford in Hertfordshire for many years. They had four daughters and a son, and emigrated to Australia in the sixties. Sadly their second daughter Denise died of cancer.

Although Beryl was a brave young girl, she was only twelve when she left. How frightened she must have been to make the long train journey, from Tenby to Bolton in Lancashire, on her own. She must have had to change trains at least twice, and as she was a slow reader at school this must have been a handicap. Having reached the Bolton destination, she would still have to get a Chorley bus and get off at 'Bob's Smithy,' a pub. Then walk a mile along a country road which led over the fields to the cottage where mother was living.

Fate takes a hand in all our lives, and Beryl was sixteen when she started courting John Wilson, a farmer's son from a neighbouring farm. He was just eighteen, had never had a girlfriend before. They married three years later, and were getting on quite well, both working and buying a nice house when Beryl became pregnant.

We didn't know until after the birth that John had put some pressure on her during pregnancy to have the baby aborted. Beryl refused to do this. She had always doted on babies, and looked after as many as possible, just for the pleasure of it. She felt John would feel better about it when the baby came and he could hold it. Although she knew the thought of it was repugnant to him. As when she had tried to get him to explain his feelings about it. He had just said: "Why don't you like snakes?"

When her birth pains started, John took her into hospital, then went home and spent the night at their home. Then up at 5 am as usual he went the few miles to his parents' farm. When his parents came down to their early breakfast, he was sitting in the farm kitchen with his head in his hands.

His mother asked him: "What's wrong, is Beryl alright?"

He jumped up from the chair and said: "She's alright, she's had the baby, it's a boy. Do you want it?"

They were naturally taken aback, and when he went outside, they thought as usual he had gone to the shippon to start the milking machines. Later they were to find him in the barn, where he had shot himself through the head with an old gun, used to kill vermin on the farm. He was a tall blond-haired boy, only twenty-four. It was a desperate tragedy for all of us.

When Beryl's baby boy, who was John's double, was three she met and married a very loveable Irish boy, Martin Halpin, who adopted Alan legally as his own. They also have a daughter and son of their own, and have had a long and happy marriage.

I don't remember the time lapse between Beryl leaving and Alan and I being told that we were to go. I know it was the summer holidays from school, Alan was eight and I was ten.

Joan Jenkinson had talked to us many times of her life in Barrow-in-Furness. We had never been further afield than Pembroke Dock once on the train, and Saundersfoot where we sometimes walked.

All of a sudden we were to leave Tenby, and go to live with Joan Jenkinson's parents. We were too strictly brought up to question this. We listened to what we were told and behaved accordingly.

Somehow our nice furniture was sold. Mr Fecci bought our bedroom suites for his daughter Rosie who was getting married. They had been well polished with Mansion Polish over the years, and good wood furniture was hard to come by because of the War.

Early afternoon on our final day, we walked to the station with our cases. What they contained was all that was left of our life, as it had been.

Trains in those days had corridors, which ran from carriage to carriage, you could walk the length of the train through adjoining doors. Alan and I stood in the corridor, so that we could lean out of the window.

As the train slowly pulled away from Tenby Station and we passed over the viaduct's arches and came to the Jubilee. Our friends had come to the fence to wave us off, Wendy Knowles, John and Tony Pilson. And suddenly the sadness of it engulfed me, and the pain in my heart, left a scar that has never healed, even fifty years on. I still can't relate it without being upset. They say when you haven't a lot, you haven't got much to lose. But our loss had nothing to do with money and it was tremendous.

We were quiet and lost in our thoughts, for the rest of the journey. Behind us our dearly loved friends and our way of life. Gone our mother and sisters. Before us the unknown.

Midway I know we changed at Crewe and dad gave us a threepenny bit each to get a chocolate bar from the Fry's machine on the platform. It was early morning the next day when we arrived at our destination. Joan's mother's flat, we has never seen anything like it before, and hope not to again. Row after row of tenement red-brick buildings, with flights of stone steps and iron railings leading up to each flat; three stories high, each unit six flats.

Mr and Mrs Richardson were kindly people. He was an engine-driver for the railway, and took us for a ride in the big steam engine, we were allowed to put some coal on the red-hot fire, and pull the whistle handle. She was an excellent housewife, very clean. We were given the use of one bedroom, which had two single beds. Alan and I slept in one and dad in the other. Mr and Mrs Richardson had the other bedroom and Joan slept on the sofa in the only living room. There was a small kitchen, small outside yard with railings and a toilet. So the kitchen sink and enamel bowl were the only wash places. All seemed strange and prison-like to us.

September was here and we started school. Alan's was just around the corner. Mine the local Grammar was a very grand place, set in rolling grounds and two bus-rides away. The first bus-ride took me over the Barrow-in-Furness ship building docks, the bridge often had to be closed and lifted to allow big ships to pass through. This caused delays and put me in a panic, as I had another bus to catch, and I hated the thought of being late for school. So I used to get up and start off very early. I had been told that if the dockyard hooter went off, and I was near the bridge, I was on no account to walk over the bridge. As the dockers surged out en masse, and a child would be trodden underfoot, or lifted bodily over the bridge. Very frightening for a little girl from Tenby, where I knew every street and pavement, and even in Wartime feared nothing.

My father had taken me to see the headmistress and enrol me at school, but from then on I was on my own.

Fortunately in a way it didn't last long, as my father had obviously hoped to find work to keep us and find a place to live. But it seemed he was not able to do this. The Labour Exchange declared that he was too highly skilled, for them to fit to a job. He could not have anything lesser, as someone else with less skills would need it.

At the same time there was a housing shortage. Local men home from the War, were having to live in with their parents for anything up to three years before they qualified for a council house. What hope for us, aliens from Wales. Some were living in disused Nissen huts left by the Army in various states of decay.

My father had the forethought to bring mother's silver cutlery canteens and these he gave to Mrs Richardson as payment for our board, when his money ran out. Obviously this couldn't go on. The strange happenings in our lives came one after the other.

Suddenly one morning we were to pack our belongings and go to our mother. Why we didn't even have a suitcase I don't know, but dad packed our few clothes into a grey blanket and made a bundle of it. We said goodbye to Mrs Richardson and Joan, and walked off to Barrow with dad carrying our bundle on his back.

We went to the lorry depot where dad had arranged for a lorry-driver to give us a lift, as far as Wigan in Lancashire his destination. I remember he had some fingers missing from one of his hands. Dad sat in the front of the cab with the driver, and Alan and I and our bundle were put in the back of the open lorry.

We had never travelled in a lorry before, and we were very unsure and frightened. We seemed to be travelling most of the day. Through small north-country towns, the houses and shops were mostly of dark stone. One or two factories were royal blue, where the royal blue powder they manufactured to be used as a laundry whitener had seeped into the stonework of the factory walls.

When we reached Wigan the lorry-driver dropped us at the bus station where we got a bus to Bolton. I don't remember having anything to eat or drink on this journey. At Bolton we had to get another bus to Chorley, dad asked the driver if he would put us off at the 'Bob's Smithy' public house, Smithills.

How different from Barrow-in-Furness now, apart from this pub and a few adjoining cottages there was nothing else in sight, except a long straight road leading between the fields which were bounded by dark-grey and black stones. In Wales all our hedgerows were full of flowers at all seasons. As children we rejoiced in them so much.

Like little aliens we walked this road, with our pathetic bundle, and unhappy father. After about a mile we saw a farm and a group of grey stone cottages. My father told me to go and ask an old gentleman, who was sitting in his garden, the way to Walkers Fold.

"Excuse me, please sir," I said. "Could you tell me the way to Walkers Fold?"

"*Aye lass,*" he replied. "*It's dan yon, ore brow. Ye can just see the roofs from 'ere.*"

I memorised it distinctly and repeated it to my father, although it seemed a foreign tongue to me, as I did French and Latin at school.

We walked a little further together, and then my father said: "Right, I'll say goodbye to you now. You go down to those cottages there and ask for your mother, who is now called Mrs Greenwood. I'll wait here for a while and if you don't come back I'll know you're alright."

He kissed us, which he had never done, and his last words to me were: "If you are not able to be a schoolteacher, be a police woman." He had high hopes for me, my dad. I never saw him again.

Alan and I knocked on the first cottage door. A white-haired lady answered, and I politely asked where Mrs Greenwood lived. She directed us to a small cottage in the farmyard. We pushed open the gate, liked the pretty leaded windows as we walked past. Knocked on the brown wooden door, and fell into our mother's arms.

BUILDING ON SHIFTING SANDS

The first thing we did at the cottage, number four Walkers Fold, Smithills, was have a bath. Quite a nice bathroom had been made in what had obviously been a small bedroom. As you sat in the bath you could see down the steep clough of land at the back of the Fold.

Quite picturesque in a rugged way. The grassy hill fell to a stream with a little bridge across it for the road, which the Fold was situated on.

The other side of the stream rose in height and this was wooded, and then there were fields where the land levelled out running into heath covered moorland.

From Walkers Fold itself, a group of five properties, no other houses were visible.

We had something to eat as it was early evening, midsummer. The living room of the cottage was oblong and quite attractive as it had a very pretty leaded window with a wide sill. My mother had several geraniums flowering. There was a large open stone fireplace at one end, black beams on the ceiling and a small narrow kitchen went off at the other end. An under-the-stairs cupboard was used as a pantry and upstairs two double bedrooms and the bathroom.

My mother's partner, Tom Greenwood, was now referred to as our stepfather. To give him the credit he was due as he kept us as if he was our father, from time to time. And was never on any occasion unkind to us. When you consider we could have been placed in care, we have to be very grateful for what we were given. In difficult circumstances, when we were still of an age to be dependent. I was thirteen, Alan was eleven.

Beryl was already with mother as she had come here after running away from home in Tenby. She was so pleased to see us, and as soon as we had washed-up we went off to explore the surrounding countryside.

Compared with Barrow-in-Furness this was heaven. But of course it was strange, and now we had found our mother after an absence of three years, we had lost our father.

A footpath led through the Fold and following the line of the stream it led to a sort of sunken village, Barrow Bridge, with the stream babbling through its stony course. All the cottages set up on a bank were dark grey and blackened stone. There was a shop, which was a general store, post office and cafe, and Beryl bought us a glass of the local delicacy - Vimto and Sarsaparilla. Something we had never tried before and it was delicious.

Beryl had managed to get a job, nanny to a baby boy, Martin Kippax, who lived in the next cottage to us, much bigger than ours. It had three reception rooms. These people were wealthy mill owners, as were the people who my mother worked for as a cleaner. The Omerods.

The cottage that we were now living in was a tied-to-the-job place, part of her wages. Their detached house, the first in the Fold, had a large garage for their veteran cars and a beautiful sunken garden.

The middle two houses in the Fold were a farmhouse and farm cottage belonging to the Bolton family. Mr Bill Bolton, farmer, and Mrs Bolton had four children: Billy, David, Freddie and baby Josephine. The farm cottage was occupied by old Mr Bolton and his second wife.

The ground outside the walled gardens was the actual farmyard. The hayloft, barn and shippon, as they called the cow byre, were all only about twenty feet away.

Ducks and hens quacked and clucked around your feet. Geese and pigs nosed your pockets for titbits. Cows and horses came and went. The big bull was safely bolted up most of the time, thank goodness!

Alan was in his element with all these animals and he made loving friends with one of the sheepdogs, Jill. It seemed mother was still doing her midwifery work. Now delivering baby piglets and calves to help the farmer.

Even as slightly older children you don't really concern yourself with your parents' problems. You only see what is obvious and what concerns you.

Living with a man you were not legally married to at this time was a degrading and highly frowned on matter. Bad enough if you were independent, but my mother was not and did not wish to offend her employers (very pious people) with her position as it involved the roof over our heads.

She had answered an advertisement in a newspaper for the job. How she came to be in this area I do not know. At the time of it being granted to her there was just her and Tom. He was a good, hardworking man. He has been working for the Ministry of Trade during the War. At one period he had the gruesome task of digging bomb victims out of their shattered homes in the London Blitz. He was a tall, well-built Scotsman with handsome features. Apart from his liking a pint in a pub, my mother and his work were his whole life.

He turned his hand to improving and redecorating the cottage, with the owner's permission, and they gladly paid for the materials. Impressed by his work they asked him to do work for them. He did already have a full-time job, but this extra work was done in the evenings and weekends.

Just settling to some extent, they first had Beryl arrive out of the blue. Then Alan and I arrived. If my mother was to house us, explanations were necessary. My mother and Tom went over to the Omerods one evening, soon after our arrival, and discussed the matter openly.

The Omerods were religious people of the Lancashire upper class. Mill owners in the affluent cotton industry which was booming at this time, the late 1940s, but was soon to fall into decline due to the imported cheaper cottons from Hong Kong.

They had a rigid code of behaviour for themselves as well as others. I cannot call them ungenerous, as they certainly were not to me, but my mother found them parsimonious, as they would even save half a spoonful of mashed potato left from one day to the next rather than waste it.

However, it seems they heard my mother out and then not unkindly said: "Well Nancy," my mother's name was Annie but they saw fit to change it, "one thing you can be sure of in life is that your sins will always find you out! And you must remember a rolling stone gathers no moss!"

My mother and Tom returned to the cottage to await the outcome and to carry on as normal until then. Mr and Mrs Omerod would have been, I suppose, in their early seventies. A devoted, handsome couple. They had bought their country house for their retirement. They had one spinster daughter in her late forties living at home, and a housekeeper-cook, Miss Hood, who would have been in her sixties. My mother was engaged to do the housework and take the burden of the work off the older ladies. It was a five-bedroom house. Very lovely.

Discussing this meeting, my mother felt that being such a small community it would be better for all concerned if the other neighbours were put in the picture, so to speak. So Beryl went and told the Kippax's and I told Mrs Bolton at the farm.

Mrs Bolton was a Catholic and divorce to her was an anathema. But she said she understood and it was no way the fault of the children. She would appreciate it if we could come over whenever possible and help her with the babies, and as the nearest school was some five miles away, Alan

BUILDING ON SHIFTING SANDS

and I could go in the milk van with Billy and Freddie each morning when her husband took the milk.

The morning following the meeting, Miss Omerod and Mr Omerod came to the cottage. They said they would like to speak to Tom about putting up a partition across the largest bedroom so that Alan, being a boy, could have his own room. This was a very generous gesture, an acceptance of the situation so to speak. They all went upstairs to discuss the alterations.

My mother did ask me if I still wanted to go to Grammar School when the September term started. It was some ten miles away and involved the daily bus fare on four buses to get there and back, to say nothing of the cost of new uniform. I was old enough to know that it wasn't feasible, so I said: "No mum, I'll just go to the ordinary school until I'm fifteen and then I can work and keep myself."

For a while we were quite happy there. The children from the neighbouring farms, all boys, joined us for games of rounders in a field, or, up to our old tricks, we lit a fire down by the stream and sat around while I told them stories of our life in Tenby which they never seemed to tire of.

Now, who comes next to the cottage door? Peggy and her husband Bert Overthrow. They had been working and living in a hotel in Malvern, Worcester, as a cook and chambermaid. Peggy had become pregnant with twins. The umbilical cord from one baby became twisted around the other baby's neck. Both babies died and aborted at six months pregnancy.

Peggy was obviously very ill and couldn't continue her job as she was also very upset. Naturally she wanted to come to her family. She had kept in touch with mother by letter, so she came to Walkers Fold.

Once again my mother was put in a very difficult position. The family was getting larger and the possibility of keeping the cottage was getting less. Beryl was allowed, by the

Kippax's to sleep in. She could then see to baby Martin, who adored her, in the night if he woke.

I moved into the tiny bedroom with Alan: one single bed and a chair. Both fairly small we slept one each end of the bed and I read him poetry about "Old Uncle Tom Cobley and All," which he loved.

Peggy and Bert had the second bedroom and bought a new bedroom suite for it. What the Omerods thought of all this I don't know. Whatever next? Peggy, still extremely pretty, was not well. She went back and forth to the doctors with an awful cough. On one visit it was his locum who sent her for an X-ray. It was confirmed that she had tuberculosis, which was a killer in those days, and she went into a sanatorium on Boxing Day and was there for two years.

Thanks to this doctor and because of the overcrowding at the cottage, Peggy and Bert were given a council house; hard to get at this time as so many needed rehousing after the War. It was some fifteen miles away. A very nice semi-detached house with large garden, and when they took it over, mother, Tom and Alan went with them. Beryl stayed with the Kippax's and I stayed with the Bolton's. To earn my keep after school, weekends and holidays: washing, ironing, cooking, cleaning, minding the babies.

They were a kind family and Mrs Bolton, often alone as her husband worked long hours, was glad of the female company which I provided. I shared my bedroom with David who was two. Chubby and blond curls he was one of those babies who make you laugh just to look at them. He was only a year old when baby Josephine was born so had to share his mother to a great extent. He loved me because I made up games for him. He once got his head stuck between the bars of the brass bedstead. Gosh, he did frighten us, until I instinctively felt I should push his head down to the mattress and quickly pull it through. I had no experience of this, but it did the trick.

I got on well at school. My teaching in Tenby put me ahead of the pupils in the Lancashire Catholic School, so I seemed to come top in most subjects. My Pembrokeshire accent was appreciated by my headmaster, who came from Fishguard, so I was asked to go on stage for narration, plays and poetry.

This Catholic School, Saint Edmund's, was self-supporting and it was entirely due to the headmaster that Alan and I were allowed to attend.

We were not obliged to go to the religious mass, being Church of England, but I felt it was manners to go and indeed found it quite beautiful in many ways. All at the school were extremely kind to us.

I was given unexpected praise on one occasion when the headmaster, speaking after mass one morning, remarked that he was interested to see that the only person in time for mass was me, a non-Catholic, and he thanked me for setting an example! I never could bear to be late for anything, so got up early and left before the milk van, walked a mile and half to the bus-stop and got to school early.

Any free time from our obligations at Walkers Fold, Beryl and I went out together visiting mother, Alan, Tom and Bert or Peggy, who was still in hospital and only allowed to wave from a distance as her illness was infectious. But she was making a recovery. Her lung had been collapsed and was kept down by air injections until the cavity healed.

Still fond of going to the pictures, Beryl used to treat me on a Saturday out of her wages. She only earned fifteen shillings a week, plus her keep.

We walked to the bus-stop and got the bus into Bolton, bought some broken biscuits from Woolworths to share as a treat, and Beryl, now being sixteen, scorned the front row, so we went in the one-and-nines. Very posh!

When walking home from school, Alan and I had made friends with the other children who lived out on the moors. One fair boy Dennis Wilson wanted to be my boyfriend and used to hold my hand as we walked along. One day Beryl had come to meet us pushing baby Martin Kippax in the pram. She laughingly said to Dennis: "You are a nice young boy! Any more like you at home?" It was a remark she had heard used in Tenby as soldiers looking for a sweetheart were apt to say this to young girls like ourselves, and we loved to watch their expressions when we said: "Yes, six!"

One Saturday evening, coming home from the pictures we were just stepping off the bus and there across the road, sitting on a bench by the bus-stop, was Dennis and his older brother, John. A taller version. Country boys to the soles of their feet.

They had just finished milking the cows and wore black berets pulled down across their foreheads to keep their skin and hair off the cows' hides. They had their work clothes on and great big 'wellies' with the tops turned down. As both boys were platinum blondes with very fair skin, their faces looked quite ghostly.

Beryl and I froze for a moment before crossing over. Both having the same sense of humour we really wanted to fall about laughing. She squeezed my hand and whispered: "Avis, I think this is our first date!" Not a bit like Errol Flyn at the pictures!

We went around as a foursome for a while. I was too young to think much of romance, except that I felt it was nice to have a special friend who wanted to be with me, but Beryl married her country boy and several years later Dennis was to join me as Godparents to their son she called Alan. I have previously related the tragic events surrounding his birth.

Considering the dramatic changes in our lives, we had adjusted well, and although separated from most of our family we were not unhappy, making the most of each day, as we all must do.

But change was again blowing in our direction. My mother and Tom had gone to the Isle of Man to live. Tom had work interests there and the opportunity had arisen. Peggy was now at home from hospital. But she was still delicate and was to be an out-patient for the next year or two. Mother left Alan with Peggy. Beryl and I didn't even get to say goodbye to her.

We visited Peggy for discussion. Peggy said she couldn't expect her husband to keep Alan, but she wanted to keep him and couldn't work herself because of her illness, so it might be best if we came and lived with them. Beryl could get a better-paid job and contribute to the housekeeping and I would be working within a year and could also help.

So this is what we did. But once again, it wasn't to last long as mother sent for Alan and a year later Beryl married John Wilson, and I also left for the Isle of Man.

My mother had sent me the Manx newspaper and told me to apply for a job in the hotel trade so that I would be able to 'live in' and be earning at the same time. Having been at the Bolton's in this capacity it was at least something I knew I could do.

I had a reply from my first application. A Mrs Corlett, who owned a guest-house taking thirty visitors, wanted someone young and willing to work as a waitress and chambermaid. She had recently had a hip operation and had two little girls.

After my train and ferry fares were paid I had one-pound ten-shillings. My entire possessions were in a medium suitcase. I was just sixteen. Peggy wasn't well enough to see me off. Bert was at work, so now I was on my own.

Living in Tenby doesn't prepare you for a lot of things that you encounter elsewhere. Places like big railway stations and huge docks seem frightening and confusing when compared with a homely town like Tenby where you knew every inch.

When I got off the train at Liverpool, I asked the direction for the Isle of Man steam-packet. I walked to save the bus fare and it wasn't very far, but the city traffic was something I wasn't used to. It made me realise how lucky I was not to have to live amongst this all my life, whatever my problems.

Lots of seamen down by the docks. I was directed to a glass-covered waiting area and took a seat to wait to board the Isle of Man steam-packet vessel 'Mona's Queen.' This was to take me ninety miles across the Irish Sea to the Isle of Man, known as 'Mona's Isle.'

Amid a lot of noisy activity with chains rattling, hooters sounding and engine props turning, I embarked up a steep wooden ramp.

The boat was quite luxurious with lots of upholstery and varnish. All the crew wore sailors' uniforms; their hats had 'I.o.M' on them. Going into the lounge area of the steerage section I met a girl I knew from Bolton. Her name was also Mona. She came from the Isle of Man and had gone to Bolton to find work to save up as she was now going home to marry her boyfriend.

We had a four-hour crossing in front of us so we had a hot drink and a sandwich. It made such a difference having someone to talk to. She was a few years older than me. She told me about the island. It was thirty-six miles long and eighteen miles wide. She said she knew where I was going to work and gave me her address in case I needed a friend.

It was a bright and breezy day and I wasn't seasick. The boat had to turn, quite well out, to come in to the island and all the passengers collected their suitcases and stood by the rails to see the island appear.

What a remarkable experience. In the foreground, set in the sea, was a small rock with a miniature castle on it. The sea front of Douglas stretched in a wide crescent of golden sand. The wide esplanade had horse-driven trams running along it and the pastel coloured hotels were built from one end to the other. Set about them in the cliffs were white castles and forts amid green trees.

I looked forward hopefully to this strange and beautiful island. Today was the first day of the rest of my life.

HAPPY REUNIONS

One of the nicest things about living in Tenby is that each generation are able to make friends with the children of their parents' friends, and so the love and closeness go down from one era to the next.

Because of my written work appearing in the Tenby Observer local newspaper I have had the wonderful experience of being reunited with some of my old-time friends after an absence of fifty-three years. Amazing to say in the least, and they have welcomed me back into their lives and homes as if it was just last week that I left.

One fine man, Fred Lewis, of Heywood Court off Heywood Lane, Tenby, was at school with my older sisters and went on himself to be a crew member of the Tenby Lifeboat in the 1950s and 60s.

My father, Alfred Cottam, served on the Tenby Lifeboat in the 1930s and 40s with his father Ted Lewis, and his uncle Bertie Lewis. All three were together for the **Fermanagh Rescue**. At this time I was only two years old and Fred Lewis was fourteen, so he has some firsthand memories of the event and of other things not recorded in our historic reference works, which I will relate to you.

Fred Lewis, son of Tenby Lifeboatman Ted Lewis, was born in the grounds of the Tenby Museum on the Castle Hill in 1924. His mother was one of the caretakers of the museum. His father was one of eleven children born to Thomas Snell Lewis and Mary Lewis at number ten Harbour Flats, Bridge Street, Tenby. Fred's uncle Bertie was also born there. As one of such a big family, when Bertie left school he left Tenby to find work. He went to the coal mining area of Bargoed, in the South Wales' valleys, where he fell in love and married a local girl called Hilda. They eventually returned to Tenby and lived at number eight

Harbour Flats, next to Bertie's old home, and both Bertie and Ted were members of the Tenby Lifeboat crew.

At the outbreak of the War in 1939 both the brothers joined the Royal Navy. Bertie attained the rank of Petty Officer, serving for the six years duration of War.

Ted won the Distinguished Service Medal during his War Service, which was presented to him at Buckingham Palace by King George VI.

Another of their brothers Dennis Lewis was also a crew member on the Tenby Lifeboat. Unfortunately he died in 1966.

After the War in 1945 Bertie took up his sea-work and his Lifeboat crewmanship. He did the Caldey Run taking visitors 'to and fro' from Tenby Harbour to see Caldey Island and its monastery.

My sister Joyce has fond memories of Bertie and Hilda as she used to call at their flat and take their golden retriever dog for a walk. Many years later she was to return to Tenby with her husband and three sons and was on Bertie's boat going over to Caldey.

Bertie wouldn't take the passenger money as he said, "No, you are Alf Cottam's family." It made my sister cry as our father had never met any of his grandchildren.

I was about three when I went to Bertie and Hilda's flat one summer's evening with both my parents, which was unusual. Hilda and Bertie joined us for a walk on the North Beach and Bertie picked me up and carried me on his shoulders. I had never experienced a ride like this before. He was a tall handsome man. I felt as big as Goscar Rock, the big rock stack in the middle of the North Beach. Bertie and Hilda were unable to have children of their own. Lovely people that they were, they loved others.

Fred remembers them with great fondness as they treated him as a son and he spent a lot of time with them and still misses them. Fred can remember the day my father, Alfred Cottam, came to the Tenby Lifeboat Station. He can remember his father, Ted Lewis, telling him: "We've got a busy day tomorrow, the new Lifeboat Mechanic is coming." Fred was nine years old; at this time I was not born.

Fred's memories of the **Fermanagh Rescue** - the ship's Master, Captain Hoy, was cast away in the ship's boat and lost. The ship's cat was also lost. Each member of the Tenby Lifeboat crew was presented with a silver watch and chain, and the sum of £5, raised by public subscription. The following is the inscription on the silver watch presented to Tenby Lifeboat Mechanic, Charles Crockford's father:

> TENBY LIFEBOAT
> *PRESENTED BY*
> *PUBLIC SUBSCRIPTION*
> *TO* JAMES N CROCKFORD
> *FOR SERVICES RENDERED TO*
> SS FERMANAGH
> BELFAST
> 15-1-1938

Bertie and Ted Lewis were part of the crew. Bertie lost part of one of his fingers in this rescue.

Bertie and Ted passed away in their beloved Tenby and are buried in Tenby cemetery.

Fred also remembers in 1953 when the same Tenby Lifeboat, the *John R Webb II*, was launched to the **Saint Govan's Lightship Rescue** in a force 10 gale. Crew members were: Coxswain Tommy 'Josh' Richards, Second Coxswain Bertie Lewis, Bowman William 'Billy Ila' Thomas, Mechanic William Rogers, Second Mechanic Dennis Lewis, Henry 'Sheriff' Thomas, Tommy 'Dowie' Howells, Dennis Walters and Brian Lewis. Coxswain Richards made three attempts to come alongside the vessel, so that all crew members of the lightship were able to jump aboard the Lifeboat and so were saved.

The **Kilo Rescue** in 1963. Fred remembers that the Tenby Lifeboat, *Henry Comber Brown*, was launched just before one o'clock in the morning in a Force 10 gale. The *Kilo* was carrying a highly inflammable cargo which had caught fire in the hold.

The crew of the Lifeboat were powerless to help the stricken vessel as they had lost the use of one of their engines and had no option but to make for Swansea.

The Mumbles Lifeboat was launched and was able to escort the *Kilo* to Swansea Bay where she ran aground and the Lifeboat took off her crew.

The Tenby Lifeboat crew were: Coxswain William Thomas, Second Coxswain Ivor Crockford, Fred Lewis, Flanagan Crockford, Patrick Crockford, Billy Parcel, Billy 'Bun' Davies, Mechanic Leslie Day.

After my **Tenby Lifeboat Station Sacred Ground** letter [refer to first chapter of this book] was published in the Tenby Observer in October 1998, I received a surprise telephone call. I had just come in the front door of my house after a weekend away and the telephone was ringing in the hall.

A lady with the Pembrokeshire accent said: "Avis Cottam?"

I said, "Yes!"

"Margaret Warner here, now King. I saw your wonderful letter in the paper so I gave the Tenby Observer a ring and asked them for your number. I thought I'd ring to say hello as we were in school together."

Well I was amazed. Margaret and I went back to 1943 – fifty-five years ago when we were in Standard Three at Tenby Council School, Ensor Morgan's class.

Living down on the Quay at that time the children within the town walls tended to go to the National School [closed in 1951] in Upper Park Road but in 1943 some of the pupils were transferred to Tenby Council School. Although their friends came with them, they were then to make friends with the rest of the school children in the town.

The War had been on for four years and our classrooms' windows had strips of brown paper in cross-work patterns over them in case of bomb-blast. Our playground had a big air raid shelter in it [which is still standing and can be seen below the main entrance in Greenhill Road] but, fortunate as we were, we only went in it for practise when the school bell rang and we all filed out in an orderly line.

Margaret, like myself, was small, thin and brown. As I was a child of 'The Woodland' it being on my doorstep, so to speak, so Margaret was a child of 'The Harbour,' and like me she lived as much as possible in the great outdoors of the Quay, the Castle Hill, the beaches and the caves. What a wonderful playground for children who were free to roam and play. Our strict discipline within our upbringing and schooling ensured to the fullest extent possible that we should be sensible enough to guard our own safety in any situation. We were naturally acute to danger as we honed in through constant familiarity with our environment, looked after ourselves, learning all the time from our elders.

Margaret and her family lived at number two Harbour View, Crackwell Street, Tenby. Her sister Beryl was a few years older and was friends with my older sisters Barbara, Peggy and Joyce.

As young ladies they would join up to go to the dances at the De Valence, with another young lady like themselves, one of the Thomas', I think it was Vi for Violet. I can remember going with them to call for her to join them to go to the dance. I was to go home when they went in and I was wishing I were ten years older so I could go too.

As we sat on the sofa at Vi's home on the Quay, she got ready for the dance. On her bare legs she applied 'leg tan,' a liquid make-up from a bottle, and from the back of the heel to the back of the knee she drew a long black line with an eyebrow pencil.

I was fascinated by this, as I had never seen it done before. The American influence was in vogue, and magazines showed ladies with sheer nylon stockings with black heel insets and long black seams (hopefully straight) up the back of the leg, the tops of which were fastened with suspenders that had small rubber buttons to keep them in place. As these were apt to pop off they were often replaced by a silver threepenny bit. But I digress!

These beautiful stockings were very sought after and sometimes received from American sweethearts as gifts sent from the United States in between the pages of newspapers and comics or hidden in some other way in a personal parcel as tax would have to be paid if they were declared.

As so many girls didn't have 'the real thing' so to speak the make-up adornment was a substitute. Disastrous sometimes in our Welsh rain, as once the drips from the rubber rainwear trickled down the legs and streaks of tan and black started to run it was a far from glamorous effect. What we girls do for fashion!

After our friend's legs were satisfactory, the next problem was her hair, which was not naturally curly, and most hairstyles of the day were all waves and curls. From the fire in the hearth Vi removed a pair of hot curling tongs. I had never seen these before as in our house we all had such curly hair. My mouth and eyes were wide open with wonder as she daintily spat on the tongs to test the heat. The bobble of spit sizzled and she proceeded to entwine them in a tress of hair, twisting them round and holding them for a few seconds. This formed soft curls that were attractive. I was looking forward to trying the 'leg tan,' but I didn't think I'd try the curling tongs - I'd be much too scared!

Margaret's family was the Morgan's: John, Joan and Megan. Her grandmother was a wonderful woman, kind and hardworking, the backbone of the family, keeping them together, well cared for and loved in times of hardship. Like us in a material sense they didn't have much, but they knew great happiness and fun from their wonderful environment and the closeness of their friends and family.

Margaret's grandad on her mother's side, John Brooking, was one of the Tenby Lifeboat crew in 1910. The ***William and Mary Devey*** pulling and sailing Lifeboat had been in commission at Tenby for eight years at that time.

His first rescue as a crew member was to be the **Ellen Rescue**. The Arklow Schooner *Ellen* which had begun to drag her anchor in the Caldey Roads [between Tenby and Caldey Island] during a south-westerly gale with heavy seas. The ***William and Mary Devey*** was launched just after midnight on February 21st 1910 and made good progress reaching the schooner and saved the crew of three. As they turned to leave the *Ellen*, another schooner the *John and Margaret* of Caernarfon was seen to be in grave danger and the Lifeboat returned and saved a crew of four men.

Margaret's grandfather, John Brooking and our present Coxswain Alan Thomas are related, as his grandmother was John Brooking's sister. So the Tenby Lifeboat lineage continues, and I know there must be a lot I have not been able to mention. I hope they will forgive me and realise it is not a deliberate omission, and one day perhaps, in the future I will be able to amend this when more facts come to me through my work.

As I went to Greenhill Grammar School [replaced in 1961 with Greenhill Comprehensive School situated between Heywood Lane and the Marsh Road] at the age of ten I lost touch with my little classmate Margaret. She said she missed me. The following year I was to move away during the summer holiday and none of our friends knew where we had gone. No more did we!

Margaret left our old school at the age of fifteen in 1950. She worked in 'The Milk Bar' by the 'Busy Bee' in town [junction of South Parade and White Lion Street]. Her family were rehoused, in common with a lot of old Tenby town families, to the Glebe between the Narberth Road and the Green. These council houses were just being built when I left Tenby in 1948.

When she married and had her children she moved to Heywood Court where she has been living ever since.

Thank you Margaret for welcoming me back into your life. It means more than words can say.

Whether happy or sad, our most precious time of all is our childhood.

Once again, following my **Tenby Lifeboat Station Sacred Ground** letter in the Tenby Observer, I got a letter from my little long lost friend Wendy Nowell. She was so excited. You see miracles do still happen, thanks to the power of the Press.

After an absence of fifty-three years we were reunited. Still just the same affection for each other. In tune emotionally and in our outlook in life, our interests and hobbies.

Wendy said that so many times she had wondered what had become of me and my family, as she spent so much of her time with us when little.

She has been married to John Pendell from Pembroke Dock for forty years now. They have a lovely family of son, Johnny and daughter, Janette. They are both married and each has a son and daughter and live nearby.

Wendy's husband John is a fine carpenter by trade. He did internal woodwork restoration on the Tenby Lifeboat Station and has made a beautiful glass-topped cabinet in Saint Mary's Church from special wood imported to tone in with the existing décor.

Their son Johnny bought number thirty-five the Maudlins, Gwyneth Bryn's old house, which is directly opposite Maudlin Villa [now called Windy Nook] where I was born.

As I have been back to Tenby twice in the last year [1999] Wendy and I and our husbands, and Margaret Warner and Freddie Lewis, have been able to enjoy each other's company and hope to do so many more times in the future. Friendships formed in early childhood are irreplaceable.

EPILOGUE

by Alan Thomas, Coxswain of Tenby Lifeboat
Arthur Squibbs, Honorary Secretary of Tenby RNLI
Researched by John Fish Publishers

Researching the Launching Records of the Tenby Lifeboat *RFA Sir Galahad* one is struck by the almost routine-like nature of most call-outs. For such is the dedication, expertise and efficiency of all Lifeboat crews and their shore helpers (those who man the Lifeboat Station to assist at launch and rehousing) that it is as if a well-rehearsed drama is taking place.

Twenty-four hours a day, 365 days a year, at any time the maroons may be fired that signify the launch of the Tenby Lifeboat. Two maroons are launched high over Tenby town, accompanied by a loud explosion; dogs bark, seagulls take to the air and the inhabitants of Tenby wonder ... wonder where their Lifeboat is going and when it will return. In the day a puff of grey smoke marks the explosion, due to the speed of sound being slower than the speed of light the explosion is seen before it is heard; at night the explosion is marked by a bright flash. A single maroon means a call-out for Tenby's Her Majesty's Coastguard Cliff Rescue Team.

And so the majority of call-outs are: to assist a vessel in distress, perhaps engine or some other mechanical failure or even sinking; medical emergencies due to someone being taken seriously ill on Caldey Island or an injury to the crew of a trawler; a swimmer missing perhaps swept out to sea by treacherous currents; persons cut off by the tide and stranded on rocks or beaches soon to be engulfed by the incoming sea; a missing diver; surfers, windsurfers, jet skis, sailing dinghies or canoeists in difficulty; reports of red distress flares; yachts and motor cruisers missing or overdue.

200 A TENBY LIFEBOAT FAMILY

Sometimes the Lifeboat is launched and the rescue mission cancelled when new information has been received by the Coastguard. But the sea takes no prisoners and at each call-out a life or lives is at stake. The sea with her unrivalled natural beauty can give life, can give food, work, entertainment, relaxation and enjoyment; can give death. And standing between the sea and her moods, between life and death, is the RNLI.

But then there are the rescues which catch the imagination for not only are the lives of the crew of a vessel, overcome by a storm and threatened by sinking or being run aground on a dangerous lee shore, at stake but the very lives of the Lifeboat crew. Accounts of rescues are based on Coxswain Alan Thomas' own words.

22nd September 1989: *New Venture*, *Seeker* and *Silver Stream*; fishing boats sheltering from storm; deteriorating visibility towards dusk, sea-state very rough, swell 8-9 metres, south-westerly 9. "We had just finished rehousing the ***RFA Sir Galahad*** from a call-out, and the crew had dispersed, when the Swansea Coastguard phoned Tenby Lifeboat Station. Three fishing boats from Ilfracombe were sheltering in Rhossili Bay, 16 miles away across Carmarthen Bay on the Gower Peninsula, but due to the southerly gale veering westerly were now in grave danger. I immediately fired the maroons and within minutes the crew had returned and the Lifeboat was launched ... Before we could reach the casualties *Seeker* had suffered engine failure and run aground, her crew were rescued by an RAF rescue helicopter from Chivenor ... An hour after launch we reached Rhossili and I ordered the crew out on deck with lifelines clipped to safety-rails, and steered from the duplicate controls on the centre-deck aft of the main cabin. As ten metre waves were plunging us chest deep in seawater we spied *New Venture* and *Silver Stream* through the spray under the cliffs of Worms' Head ... The trawlers were caught between the lee shore of the beach and the massive waves out to sea, attempting to keep their position within the bay by alternatively fighting their way out to sea then surfing back towards the beach. Then out to sea I saw an enormous wave ... It caught *Silver Stream* broadside on capsizing her but then as we approached her she rolled back. Her sole crew was trapped in the wheelhouse but managed to escape through a window and, as I held the *RFA Sir Galahad* in position, Roy Young and my brother Clive Thomas managed to haul him onboard. Our attention now turned to the *New Venture* and we were eventually able to shepherd them back home to Tenby."

*Lifeboat crew: Coxswain Alan Thomas, Mechanic Charles Crockford, Clive Thomas, Roy Young, Denny Young, Steve Crockford, Bobby James. The RNLI awarded its Silver Medal and the Maud Smith Award to Coxswain Alan Thomas, with the rest of the crew all being awarded 'Letters of Thanks.' A painting of this rescue may be viewed at the **Hope and Anchor** Public House, Saint Julian's Street, Tenby.*

31st March 1994: Boat missing, 18 foot power boat; rain, fair visibility, sea-state very rough, swell 6-7 metres, south-westerly 8-10. "A boat was overdue from Laugharne ... we got up to the 'Carmarthen bar' at 21:30 ... we were in rapidly shoaling water and very rough seas when the Coastguard informed us that the casualty had been found and so we were to return to Tenby - which we very gratefully did."

Lifeboat crew: Coxswain Alan Thomas, Mechanic Charles Crockford, Graham Waring, Denny Young, Mac Waring, Daniel Thomas, Kevin Lewis.

26th June 1994: *Nimrodel*, 18 foot cabin cruiser, lost rudder; rain, moderate visibility, sea-state rough, swell 2 metres, south-westerly 5-6. "Vessel off Pendine Beach, another boat was attempting to tow her clear but conditions were overpowering them ... on reaching them they had closed to the beach just inside the surf. The *Calambad* slipped her

202 A TENBY LIFEBOAT FAMILY

tow-rope and we passed our tow-rope to the casualty, and towed her out into deeper water. We then crossed the 'Carmarthen bar' and took her up the River Towy to Llanstephan. There were two people onboard and two dogs, *all* were wearing life-jackets."
Lifeboat crew: Coxswain Alan Thomas, Mechanic Charles Crockford, Roy Young, Mac Waring, Daniel Thomas.

20th November 1997: *Sipsmior*, 9 metre yacht, lost and overcome by conditions; overcast, good visibility, sea-state rough, swell 4-5 metres, easterly 8-9. "A yacht with two people onboard was lost in Carmarthen Bay, thought to be three miles south of Tenby, they had lost their chart overboard. After launching the Coastguard told us that the casualty was now thought to be east of Tenby and we were now west of the Woolhouse Rocks, which had not quite been cleared by the falling tide. We sighted them about three-quarters of a mile east-north-east of the rocks and carried on south to clear the rocks then headed for the casualty ... went alongside and put crewmen Denny Young and Graham Waring aboard. The occupants gave the helm to our crew and said they wanted to get off right away. They were very seasick, exhausted and frightened. They had only been able to steer downwind and were heading for the Woolhouse Rocks, which had just started to show. I told our crew to head her up to pass to the north of the rocks. Once clear we went in alongside and picked up the two occupants. They were desperate to get ashore but conditions were too bad to land until mid-evening, so they were made comfortable and reassured by the Mechanic."
*Lifeboat crew: Coxswain Alan Thomas, Mechanic Charles Crockford, Denny Young, Graham Waring, Clive Thomas, Mac Waring, Steve Crockford, Philip John, Richard Collins. The RNLI awarded 'Letters of Thanks' to Graham Waring and Denny Young. A painting of this rescue, by Lifeboatman Denny Young, may be viewed at **Tenby Lifeboat Station**.*

EPILOGUE 203

There are 223 Lifeboat Stations run by the RNLI around the coastline of the British Isles. Six of these are in Pembrokeshire and its borders:

Angle: Tyne class Lifeboat and D-class ILB.
Cardigan: Atlantic 75 class ILB and D-class ILB.
Fishguard: Trent class Lifeboat and D-class ILB.
Little and Broad Haven: D-class ILB.
Saint David's: Tyne class Lifeboat and D-class ILB.
Tenby: Tyne class Lifeboat and D-class ILB.

Members of the public are able to visit Lifeboat Stations to regular opening hours and **Tenby RNLI** cordially invites readers of **A Tenby Lifeboat Family** to visit **Tenby Lifeboat Station**.

The cost of building a new **Tenby Lifeboat Station** is estimated to be in the region of £3.5 million and the cost of a new **Tenby Lifeboat** £1.5 million.

Readers of **A Tenby Lifeboat Family** who may wish to support the **RNLI** on a regular basis can do so by taking out a **Shoreline** membership of the RNLI. Details may be obtained from: RNLI, West Quay Road, Poole, Dorset, BH15 1XF; the annual subscription includes quarterly copies of the RNLI's **The Lifeboat** magazine. Also available is a **Storm Force** membership for young people under 16.

As a final memoir to close **A Tenby Lifeboat Family** it is perhaps fitting to recall a rescue by the Tenby Lifeboat from the days of muscle powered oars and wind driven sails.

On September 1st 1908 the Helwick Lightship, off Worms' Head on the Gower Peninsula, was in serious difficulties due to a severe west-north-west gale with the crew requiring rescue. Coxswain **Thomas Davies,** in a remarkable feat of seamanship and despite the Tenby Lifeboat *William and Mary Devey* suffering serious damage due to the severe sea conditions, reached the lightship in two hours. The crew of seven were rescued and the Lifeboat then, unable to return to Tenby due to the sea and wind conditions, and with the Lifeboat crew exhausted and suffering from exposure, set sail and made landfall at Swansea.

CYMRU AM BYTH

> *"Tenby my Tenby*
> *Jewel in Welsh Crown*
> *Your beauty has brought you*
> *Great renown "*

> *"Although fate was to take me*
> *On journeys far and wide*
> *Nowhere could replace the part*
> *That you hold in my heart "*

From the poem **Tenby** by **Avis Nixon** (née Cottam).
The complete poem can be read on the Internet in the
Star of Pembrokeshire Poetry Anthology
which is accessible from the publisher's homepage:
http://homepages.which.net/~j.fish/

The **Star of Pembrokeshire Poetry Anthology** is an online attempt to compile, in real-time, an anthology of poems with a Pembrokeshire theme and readers of **A Tenby Lifeboat Family** are invited to consider submitting entries. Full details of terms and conditions of entries are given on the Internet, accessible from the publisher's homepage, as above.

When sufficient entries have been accepted it is intended to publish the **Star of Pembrokeshire Poetry Anthology** as a title in the publisher's **Star of Pembrokeshire** series.